instability
in six colors

rachel kallem whitman

ONE IDEA PRESS  PITTSBURGH

D1285066

special thanks to artist Jessica Earhart:

Jessica Earhart (she/her/hers) is a multidisciplinary artist based in Pittsburgh, PA. Collage is her primary medium, where she finds satisfaction in its impulsivity, limitations, and as an expressive way to problem solve. She creates art as a means to understand the human experience, addressing feminist themes through surrealism. Her work has consisted of both stand-alone pieces and series, as well as 'zines and comics. When she doesn't have an x-acto knife in her hand, she can be found practicing yoga, experimenting with botanicals, or baking up a storm.

www.themedialuna.com

May 18th, 2012
wedding vows

Rachel, you help me see the world as the amazing, bright, and wonderful place it is. You have truly taught me how to love, and I cannot wait to learn everything else I am sure you will teach me through our lives together.

Spencer, I love you every day. Today is particularly special, as we stand before our family and friends, but those words, those feelings, the love I have for you, it colors my existence. Every day, I love you. I always will.

· · · · · ●

To my parents, I owe you everything. I wouldn't be here without your strength, love, and hope. Look how far I've come.

To my sisters, thanks for putting up with the middle child!

To Carrie Fisher, Marya Hornbacher, Maria Bamford, and Ellen Forney, it's really magical when you and your heroes take the same antipsychotics.

To my therapist and psychiatrist, thank you for helping me find peace no matter how many times I lose it.

instability
in six colors

When I'm manic, the world feels so unbelievably beautiful and *shattered*. And there is just such sobering, overpowering ecstasy in this awe-cracked brokenness that I can't help but feel it throbbing in my bones.

The sadness settles in the cradle of my heart, as I'm the only one charged with saving this beautiful, broken, melancholic bundle that leaves *scorch* marks in my chest. I cannot sleep because I have to stand guard all night. I am the lonely, lovely, littered watchtower.

I smile and I cry and I collapse and I laugh myself back into beautiful space. I'm b u r s t i n g with bright colors and sweet agony. I am brilliant and tortured. I'm too bright to burn out.

It feels like a hypnotic ultraviolet jellyfish has curled inside me. I'm warmed and distracted with its beautiful electricity as she wraps her stinging fingers around my soft lungs and a heart that is eager to feel a jolt that brings me back to life. I can smell the singed skin.

On nights like these, I turn off the lights and watch two videos from my childhood. *The Snowman* is a short video based off a book written by a man whose wife had schizophrenia - a crazy girl just like me. But the video has no words, just pencil drawn landscapes, skies, and the rolling ocean. It stars a little boy who builds a snowman, loves him into life, and then loses him to the sun.

There is one song sung by a choir boy, who, growing up, I thought was a girl like me, and the lyrics that are seared forever in my mind cry to me, "We're walking in the air. We're floating in the moonlit sky. The people far below are sleeping as we fly. I'm holding very tight, I'm riding in the midnight blue. I'm finding I can fly so high above with you."

And I can't stop watching this video, and I can't stop crying over the sheer splendor of this story. Loving and losing and escaping into the sky as people rest peacefully beneath you - and I cry so hard with such indulgence that my chest aches. This is my story, too. Little me learned that sometimes sadness can bring immeasurable beauty with its sorrow.

I watch a scene from *Dumbo* again and again and again because I cry so hard I think I feel God. His mother is locked up, shackles on her feet, but she weaves her trunk through prison bars and cradles her son. The bittersweet lullaby plays as she rocks Dumbo, "Baby mine, don't you cry, baby mine, dry your eyes, rest your head close to my heart, never to part, baby of mine," and I cry with my entire body.

And it feels so sumptuously beautiful that I start to die.

I stare at the screen and wipe the tears from my neck and I clasp my hands as my head pounds with *violent angel wings*, "May God break my heart so completely that the whole world falls in!" From the lips of Mother Teresa's passed on to mine to echo in God's ear.

All this rapture rips me right open. I just can't keep the k a l e i d o s c o p e in and I find markers and pens and I decorate my pale arms and soft stomach, my freckled face and long legs, and my pink chest that is absolutely pleading.

I'm covered in colors.

I turn into canvas.

I listen to sad lullabies and I think of this rickety world. And I am honored to hold such euphoria, since I am simply a crazy girl lost in divine light, even though this splendor makes me suffer.

I cry until the markers run, leaving diluted tentacles etched across my skin, and I sit on my kitchen floor feeling blessed with my burden. This grief makes me whole; it feels familiar in a way I deserve.

I sit and the tears pour out and I pull my knees to my chest because I'm exquisitely splintered and responsible for the entire world's torment.

And I would sit and cry and make my colors run forever, but my husband says it is time to see the doctor.

contents

*(Black robs you of light just as depression leaves you in the dark.
My story is best told in color. I fight to leave black behind.)*

body
relationships

ONE

hypomania

eyes closed

i was serenely gliding alongside the Allegheny River on a stretch of smooth, thick tar that lay tamed. Allegheny Boulevard was no longer riddled with snow-sponsored potholes or dotted with gravely pockmarks as the sickliness of winter had finally begun to subside. The streets were redeemed and I coasted gracefully to all of my destinations on their even black surfaces, even to places I had never purposefully planned to travel. I was swept across the city by the shine of new sleek roads that I could practically taste. If I slid my tongue along these caramel-coated licorice intersections, I imagined it would taste like solidified maple syrup. Pure, perfect, sweet streets. And the river herself was all dressed up, catching pockets of sunshine in her dainty ripples, each ebb and flow sneaking a wink at me as I drove by, her waves cresting perfectly in sync to the music leaking out of my radio. How uncanny and utterly marvelous that the waves could keep a rhythmic pace, matching the loud and soft sounds volleying between my ears - music that made me drum my fingers on the dash. Candy streets, a flirtatious river, and the loudest, lightest, loveliest tinkling melody all performing an enchanting, choreographed spectacle just for me.

As I drifted, I whispered an emphatic *thank you* to my sturdy and trustworthy chariot, my 1998 Lexus, which was gifted to me by my great aunt because she had grown too old to drive to temple. In the family, my great aunt is known as a thoughtful, generous woman, so it was no surprise that she left me countless Klezmer cassette tapes in the center console that I should "use in good health" (a kind command she probably exclaimed in Yiddish). I leaned my head back against the beige leather headrest and caught glimpses of wispy clouds darting overhead through the open sunroof. I was completely free. I could fly wherever I wanted. My hand fluttered in the tickling wind as I rested it on the open car window, sighing deeply and breathing in air glittered with sugar crystals. Life was just that sweet and I knew it was designed explicitly with me in mind. For this is the divinely coordinated beauty of my life.

I hummed contentedly. My right foot, encased in a well-loved sneaker, but arched with poise as if it were in a ballerina's silk slipper, nudged more pressure onto the gas pedal and my chariot picked up speed, just like I asked. I widened my eyes as the sublime symphony of existence blossomed around me. The billowing cool wind, the crystal air filling my lungs, music that played for the sole audience of my ears, river water twinkling for my eyes only, and glossy confident streets that left me with endless options. I was overwhelmed by these blessings. All I could do was praise the tears pooling puddles in my lashes and worship every heavy drop that decorated my cheeks. I had never felt so enraptured before. Life had never been so exquisitely blissful. My heart was bursting with such intense adoration for this cherished existence that my body soon surrendered to my miracle, and, with God's name on my glistening, smiling, pink, parted lips, I closed my eyes tightly and drove even faster.

Tiny pieces of cracked glass.
Every breath threatens to shatter these buried fibers even further.
Splinters leaving slivers of loneliness lodged in my chest.
Feeling anything too deeply threatens to deface the brittle layers of skin that imprison my jagged shrapnel.
Lacerations from being a kid.
Inside me, a minefield of memories, triggers, and souvenirs.
Like inherited sadness and panic. Like a stomach that can't unclench. Like a throat that chokes on its own. A body that shudders and struggles under the weight of a girl with scissors pressed to her skin who is now a woman living with scars, silence, and untraceable deep sighs.
I don't want to talk about it. I didn't then and I don't want to now. That's what made me good, he said.
I guess it feels better having a body stuffed with secrets than a body weakened by emptiness.

false teeth

How do you explain to your dentist why you hate flossing?

Do you start at the beginning?

When I was a kid, I was pushing my imaginary friend in a swing, and she swung back too quickly and too forcefully, so much so that when the swing connected with my face, my front tooth splintered apart.

Or do you start, instead, with a cheeky example of your adolescent dental rebellion?

My dentist suggested to my parents that we should consider getting me braces. There wasn't a medical problem, but for cosmetic reasons - to clean up that smile. I told my parents if they tried to put braces on my teeth, I'd rip those brackets right off and pull those wires right out. So, they left me with my crooked smile.

Maybe you don't hold back and you dig right in to the truth—because this issue isn't trivial.

When I was a kid, I was molested by my neighbor. He told me I always had to smile whenever I saw him, and I always did. I smiled with a forced grimace that was crammed with jagged bones.

I will be pretty for no one.
But that is probably too dark and raw.

So, instead, do you say something like, *When bipolar disorder started forcing its pathology of interference into my existence, my relationship with my teeth became even more complex.* Enamel lined with speakers and microphones, gums laced with poison implanted by shadowy forces that I couldn't see but I could sense. Teeth told to crunch on antipsychotics to keep me from flying too high or being completely buried.

My crooked teeth keep secrets from me when I'm crazy.

But diving into your history of psychosis at the dentist's office, well, that might not be the appropriate venue.

Instead, do you tell a cute and true story about your teeth and your family?

My mom and I share the same teeth. We also look alike, we laugh alike, and we hug the same. Our smiles are so similar - with our equally crowded mouths, with our matching shark teeth. Our gums adorned with teeth that lean too far one way, too far the other way, some pushing past the other teeth both forwards and backwards, but they are such unapologetically aggressive incisors that they can drag you down to the depths. If you struggle, we only clamp down harder. And we laugh unabashedly louder than anyone else because we are not ashamed of our overlapping pearly whites.

Maybe a love story would do the trick?

I always tell people that I never got braces because this kind of smile builds character. Cluttered teeth build confidence. When someone loves you, cramped teeth and all, then you know that it is real love. I say this jokingly with a self-deprecating laugh, but the truth is, I don't want to be pretty for anyone. My husband has never really noticed my teeth; he is too busy leaving kisses on my lips.

However, I bet an adorable romantic embellishment doesn't convey the seriousness of the situation. It probably doesn't provide enough of an explanation as to why you prefer to leave your teeth alone, to not interact with them as much as possible. To give them space, even if that means at the expense of pink gums.

Do you clear your throat and say, *Starting when I was molested and until I was a teenager, the easiest way to self-harm was to bite into the copper freckles on my arm?*

My white arm was the perfect surface for capturing the imprint of thirty-two jumbled fangs. Each bite was just like making a mold of my teeth because I would clamp down on my skin with such conviction that, after I blotted the blood away, you would find indentations of slants and points and marks from my own built-in bear trap. I bit through my skin when I couldn't subdue the memories, when I couldn't stop reliving the experience, or when I dissociated and drifted too far away for too long. The pain released me, I pulled away, and it was easier to breathe, easier to be in my body. I don't growl pleadingly into my arm anymore, but I still remember how it felt and why I did it.

Do you think this statement will sum it all up for my dentist?

Taking minty, glossy threads and weaving them in and out, back and forth, working them through a chaotic cluster of off-white teeth in order to help keep my gums healthy is a challenge.

It is a challenge because my teeth are not just neutral towers of calcium and dentin. They are reminders of past experiences that still hurt even though I've made my peace.

Intimate moments with my teeth and gums remind me that the next time I go crazy, I'll mistrust them for days and I'll run my fingers over their ridges and press my finger pads against their points because something sinister is buried there, and I am inconsolable until the meds kick in.

Spending time with my teeth means spending time with pain that tore my heart apart, just like the blood that spills from my gums, cut through by floss - that slick red liquid across my teeth before sliding down my sink.

Despite all of this, I do love my crowded smile. Flashing it in a mirror, seeing it in a photo, imagining it when I laugh out loud, seeing it whenever I make my mom laugh, and how my husband tells me I'm beautiful whenever I jut out my snarled underbite to make a funny face.

My brave teeth prove how strong I am, while at the same time, remind me that I can't completely escape my history, the memories, or the illness that I live with every day.

My relationship with my teeth is best explained by a long story of my experiences - details that are hard to share when the hygienist tells you to "sit back and open wide."

I hate flossing. Does it make sense now?

trading every day for
hypomania

Taking a break from my body can be both *bitter* and brilliant in every eager episode that then leaves me drenched in utter exhaustion when I finally return to this pink pile of freckled me with glasses on top. And while I'm skating, sliding, sinking on a sweet hiatus from her, I forget that I'm glued down and so I'm free to float and fly into a flurry of feelings much softer and sweeter than I've been used to lately. And light and love are there—not just lingering, but living. But after every holiday away from a fleshy anchor with duties and responsibilities and arms that fling and flap, and legs that dance and trip, and fingers snapping to my own bizarre little beats, I come back into this me and I remember that this life is mine and I should enjoy being her, living with her, but also take her seriously. Because when I escape, she often b r e a k s.

panic at the aldi

Eating is fucking hard.

Last night, my husband and I decided to check out our local neighborhood ALDI since we'd heard good things, and my beloved Whole Foods is hella expensive. I've struggled with disordered eating my entire life, and while I manage everything significantly better these days, it doesn't mean the illness has disappeared. I've just developed new coping skills and lo-o-o-o-ts of therapy has helped me improve my relationships with food, control, my body, and my sense of self-worth. But I still struggle with change, especially when my food routine is disrupted. Shopping at certain stores where I feel comfortable, buying certain foods that feel safe to eat, and sticking to certain brands that I've grown accustomed to has helped me take ownership of my eating. But last night, I felt ready to venture out into the unknown - finally ready to conquer a new grocery frontier! When we walked into ALDI, I felt confident—new place, new food, new experience—a little scary, but I felt in control. *I can have fun with this!*

That is, until I became incredibly overwhelmed by all the newness.

I had a panic attack right in front of the bottles of Mountain Frost soda (Mountain Dew's hillbilly cousin). My mental illnesses pair well with panic attacks, and panic attacks don't give you a lot of warning. One minute you're casually stocking up on knock-off Girl Scout cookies (might I suggest the caramel coconut cookies a.k.a. a surprisingly on-point and equally delicious Samoas replica), and the next you've made a mad dash to the safe harbor of your Subaru and you're popping Ativan in the passenger seat like it's your job.

Life can be overwhelming for all of us, and we all have different triggers. For some of us, it's a fear of failure, a fear of abandonment, a fear of intimacy. Eating is hard for me. I've finally accepted that there will always be some degree of struggle, but I've also learned how to forgive myself when I do have the inevitable setback. And while there will always be setbacks, there will also be progress.

I had a panic attack at ALDI and I was painfully embarrassed at first—*"That wasn't a part of my plan!"* But the thing is, panic attacks are a part of my illness, a part of my life, and thus, they're in my plan whether I like it or not. But I don't let my panic attacks derail me anymore. I won't let anorexia consume me again. I take care of myself and I'm in control as much as I can be.

Last night, I had a panic attack at ALDI, but afterwards, I went home and I ate dinner and I enjoyed it. Right now, my plan is to keep trying, be kind to myself, and go back to ALDI this weekend.

my fatness

My fatness is my favorite accessory.
Unassuming, everyday lazy t-shirts, clothes that seem uneventful,
on my bold and bouncy body come alive.
Cotton, now full of charisma with my flesh peaking out proudly.
My belly fills out the once shapeless shifts so they are now overflowing and interactive,
a tank top complete with compassionate cleavage that's soft and comforting and pleasing
to the eye.
With a fat body, there is so much to see, to touch, to taste, to love.

My fatness makes a statement.
That lifeless dress with the loud pattern hanging limply on the hanger is suddenly full of
movement when painted on my chubby frame.
The flat fabric now textured with my lumps and bumps,
a sight that you just want to sink your teeth into, and there's enough to share.
So much to desire and admire, with every wiggle, the pattern is animated into erotic energy.
Like my decorative necklace with clinking beads, I am not afraid to make noise, to be
noticed, to remind you that fat is fashionable
I don't need your permission or your approval, but I know you're looking, and you are
lucky to see me.

My fatness is intoxicating.
With clothes that cling to my curves, I stand tall and stand out.
A leopard print bra that power clashes with my pale freckles,
a tight red skirt that gift wraps my thick thighs,
my large belly leaving a smile across the taut spandex.
I am not ashamed of the space I take when I glide into the club on chunky heels.
I dance like everyone's watching, gyrating and jiggling,
triggering the earthquake emanating from my well-built middle.
A great thing about being fat is when you dance, your whole body celebrates.
With a fat body, there is so much more to hypnotize you.

My fatness does not dilute my confidence.
Loving my fatness in a world that tells me I am not enough
because I am too much is the source of my courage.
I'm everything I want to be, from my cellulite-shimmering stomach
to my substantial swinging tits, to my quivering thighs.
I exude self-love and refuse to apologize because I'm beautiful, and I belong just as much
as the next girl, no matter how big or small she may be, we all have the right to exist,
to be proud of our shapes that come in every size and color you can imagine.

My fatness is my own.
I've learned how to be that fat girl with a genuine I-don't-give-a-fuck smile,
who considers being called "fat" a compliment, no matter who says it,
taking back her body and her power.
That woman who says she is fat without feeling a twinge of shame,
who wears her fat well because she is proud of her body and how much love she gives her skin,
but as I shine in my attire and take pride in my appearance,
I know that not everyone has arrived here yet;
that, for many of us, being called "fat" is the worst slur of them all,
that calling ourselves "fat" still feels like admitting we're failures.
But you will get here.
We must be kind to our sisters, brothers, and siblings
who are still standing on shaky ground,
and reassure them that the Earth isn't collapsing beneath our feet.
It's evolving and dancing, adapting and applauding.
Your body belongs to you.
You make the rules.

My fatness is my favorite accessory. How do you love your fat?

price check
on the vestiges of youth

I missed my period in December. This wasn't really a big deal considering I have polycystic ovarian syndrome (PCOS) and thus a corresponding history of irregular periods - *glamorous, I know* - but it was still worth mentioning to my husband. For complete transparency, with my PCOS, it is not uncharacteristic for me to forgo having a period for a month or three, as well as possessing ovaries with the consistency of cottage cheese - texture, not taste (dang, bodies are weird). Furthermore, skipping my period has always been rather anti-climatic because I've been on birth control since I was sixteen, and I am religiously dedicated to taking my baby-blockers as prescribed. When it comes to my oral contraceptives, I'm regimented and disciplined, like a sexually active nun who makes educated decisions about her body.

Since the likelihood of actually being pregnant was pretty slim, I was not particularly anxious about missing my period this month, because sometimes this just happens - no real cause for alarm. I was quick to write it off. But my husband and I were getting ready to pack up and hit the road to spend the holidays with my family, and he felt like it would be better to take a pre-vacay preggo test and just be 100% sure before the holiday festivities rolled around. He was right, no harm in checking, better safe than sorry! Plus, I take a slew of potent psychiatric meds to manage my bipolar disorder, which would give an unplanned fetus a nice collection of flippers and a face full of countless eyes. Nobody wants that for Chrismukkah.

Fast forward to a week or so later when my husband and I attended a holiday party at a friend's house that happened to be right near a twenty-four-hour grocery store. While we had not originally planned to make a preg pit-stop, convenient city living convinced us otherwise. We made our exit from the party a little after midnight and bee-lined for the adjacent deserted parking lot of the sparsely populated chain supermarket. Walking confidently through the automatic doors, we tackled our first order of business: grabbing a pregnancy test. Mission accomplished. However, influenced by the side effects from generous helpings of gluten-free baked goods and a night of sampling bountiful fancy cheese plates, I took an impulsive detour through the aisles in order to grab a gallon of cookies n' cream ice cream. Everyone knows pregnancy tests are best paired with frozen desserts. With a pregnancy test and ice cream in hand, my husband and I sidled into the checkout lane.

It was just us and a very smiley, very Pittsburgh-y clerk - think feathered hair and copious Steelers talismans. I quietly watched as the pregnancy test glided slowly down the conveyor belt, followed by our midnight snack. But suddenly, an unexpected wave of embarrassment washed over me as the ice cream tub's condensation began pooling on the ambling black rubber. I realized that my pregnancy test and sweating tub of ice cream would soon be in the clutches of a self-righteous checkout lady who would fondle them, cluck disapprovingly, and shake her head with blatant disappointment because I was so irresponsible. In my head, I already heard her silent lecture and saw her judgmental glare, *So young and foolish! TSK. TSK.* Crap, here I am buying a pregnancy test with a side of consolation ice cream because I could very well be knocked up. Ruining my chances of having a bright future. *I should've known better! How could I be so reckless?* I flushed red. *Fuck, did I flush with a pregnancy glow?* That clerk was right on target. I'm a mess.

Finally, our items made it to the end of the line and I flinched as the Yinzer-ess rang them up. But she didn't bat an eye. She didn't frown. There was no I'm-giving-up-on-America's-future head shaking. No brow was furrowed in the slightest. Instead, she grinned, tilted her head while uttering a soft "Aw," as her wispy bangs rustled in the subtle grocery store breeze, and she slipped the pregnancy test into a cheap plastic bag. The made up exchange I had prematurely concocted vanished in an instant. The ice cream soon found its way into a separate bag and then she cooed, "Have an EXTRA Merry Christmas!" Without any sign of disapproval whatsoever, she handed my husband the shopping bags.

I was stunned. I felt my stomach churn with anxiety, dread, and nausea, brought on by an oh-so-sudden and completely opposite, yet equally unhappy, fresh realization. I imagine a combination of sensations most likely akin to seeing the wrong window turn pink on a pregnancy test whilst morning sickness tortures your gut. At that moment, I was shaken to the core by the unpleasant truth that I am **OLD**. I no longer qualify as a whipper snapper subject to being scolded by cashiers with old-fashioned values working at twenty-four-hour grocery stores. *Holy hell.* No one in their right mind would think I was purchasing panic ice cream on a Saturday at midnight because I had an unwanted lil' larvae squiggling in my womb. Because, by conventional standards, my husband and I are prime "aiming for a baby" candidates. We are the socially acceptable baby-having demographic. In her mind, the friendly Steeler-clad cashier rang up a pregnancy test and celebration ice cream for two competent adults, because, we are, in fact, thirty-year-old people, and thirty-year-old people want babies. That seems to be a very real trend that is probably here to stay. Damnit, I am **OLD** and **DOMESTICATED**.

While in my mind I imagined I could still pass for an easily embarrassed semi-scared teenager who had an unfortunate lapse in judgment that could potentially ruin her life and bring shame upon her family, in reality, I'm a grown ass woman. I have a stable marriage, a retirement account, a mortgage, a wicked credit score, and excellent health insurance. **I AM OLD, DOMESTICATED, AND RESPONSIBLE.** This epiphany felt worse than the gross miscalculation that I would be judged as a promiscuous delinquent. It felt like being buried under an avalanche of gallons and gallons of ice cream. *I felt old.* Having a baby now wouldn't actually ruin my life, and for a lot of people in my peer group, that is their next step towards finishing The American Dream puzzle set.

This blew my fucking mind.

For the first time in my life, I could be pregnant and it would be okay. My husband and I could (theoretically) handle it - minus that whole flipper baby thing, of course. Wow. Growing up, amiright? This took some serious time to process. Sigh. Just call me Monotonous Kallem Whitman.

So, with that, I start off 2016, not with any New Year's resolutions, but with a New Year's realization: even if I don't feel like it, to the outside world, I am an adult. And this isn't purely a good thing or necessarily a bad thing either. It just is. Time happens. I shouldn't let my age rattle me. I just need to go with it as gracefully as I can. I'm still me, but hopefully a little bit wiser now with more years under my belt. This year, I plan on continuing to be the funny, smart, spunky, and creative person I always have been, but now I'll enjoy my ice cream without worrying what other people think.

P.S. Happily married sex is fucking fantastic!

P.P.S. My snatch-ery is not a fish hatchery.

beginnings of a beautiful state of *bipolar*

There are some days when I just cry. My body is so full of feeling. And I don't exactly feel sad. And I don't exactly feel overcome with joy. I am left somewhere in the middle with my vibrant, colorful, vivacious feelings.

So suddenly, I am reminded of my heart's tremendous talent for holding on to sentimental swirling whirlpools. I become painfully aware of the lingering heaviness these feelings leave in my chest. And I realize that I feel everything so strongly and unbelievably deeply in a way that leaves me delightfully lightheaded.

And I ultimately awaken.

Because exercising complete compassion, practicing how to sit with sadness, holding—hopefully, for only a moment—a hurting heart, bursting brightly with love, light, and breeze, seeing the world as a dazzling cradle for beauty and awe, and learning how to translate self-hatred into effective outward anger makes me feel exactly like myself.

On days with unanchored tears, it is really the mere memory in my heart, my head, and my body of how deeply I can feel that renders me my Rachel.

And this brings me past the brink of my lids as I treasure the exaggerated language of my heart and, at the end, I am left at the point of overflow.

when god comes

When I was a kid, I begged for God. I remember kneeling at the corner of my bed, knees pressed into the carpet, my hands clasped together on my comforter, and as tears zig-zagged down my face, I waited for him to answer. I waited for years—and not patiently. I would cry and curse and dig scissors into my skin because the blood set me free and I was tired of waiting. Until I found God, carving notches out of my thighs and breasts was a substitute for divine cleansing. The cut would sting and seep and the pain woke me up, sending electric jolts into my brain that stabbed me awake. When the man in my neighborhood hurt me, it ripped right through me, leaving scars of shame and agony seared across my entire body. But when I clutched my silver scissors and slid them under my skin, the pain was mine and the pain was controlled. And I needed it to remind me that I wasn't a shell, I was skin and blood and bone and alive.

I kept begging for God. He spoke to so many others, and I didn't understand why I never felt him. I longed for God, I pined for God, I needed to hear his voice or I couldn't stand one more minute with all this disgust and agony festering inside of me. If God wouldn't speak to me, that meant he didn't want to save me. I couldn't exist on the power of prayer alone. I desperately needed comfort and companionship, something that would keep me safe, because my neighbor wasn't going away and I didn't know how to run.

Our conversation was born from whispers and murmurs. One day, I felt something clicking inside my skull and it sounded like softness. It felt like rhythmic purring between my ears. It felt like honey being drizzled across my brain, coating my mind with a sweetness and stickiness that kept my skull from cracking. I tried to listen to the intricacies of the echo bouncing around my head, moving into my neck, my shoulders, my chest, my stomach, my arms, legs, and feet. It felt like someone was filling in the missing colors. I was once a blob of pale nothingness, devoid of color, and now I was vibrant and alive. It wasn't drawing in between the lines, but it filled me with something significant. It took me a while but I soon realized I had found him. Or he had found me. God wrapped his arms around my mind and his embrace kept my brain from rattling so hard that it tore open the back of my skull. He stroked my body and soul and I could finally breathe without stabbing pains perforating my lungs. I didn't have to cut. I didn't have to cry anymore. Everything would be okay.

God spoke to me through his angels. Mother Teresa, Princess Diana, and Jesus took residence in my body, reinforcing the cracks that were caving in. They became the infrastructure of my skull; they erected scaffolding inside me that kept me upright - kept me together. I wasn't just skin wrapped around an aching frame, I was full of light. I would quote Mother Teresa's words in my mind: "May God break my heart so completely that the whole world falls in." It was my mantra. I recited it constantly; the soundtrack to my life and my lullaby at night. Mother Teresa sighed in my ear and told me that my suffering was by design. My pain was part of a grander plan.

Princess Diana wrapped me tightly in her laced gloves at night when I couldn't sleep. She cradled my head in her lap and ran her fingers across my forehead. I didn't need to see her because I felt her in my now quiet skull. The shadow of her love was enough to slow my breathing and soothe me while Jesus wept. He cried for me. He was my own personal martyr. He hurt so I didn't have to. If it happened at his house that day, I would lie in my bed at night and try to forget I had a body. I would try to melt into my bed, sinking so far into the mattress that it would consume me. A tomb of pillows and sheets. But when Jesus was with me, pouring tears across my chest, the pitter-patter of his pain helped assuage my own. He didn't want me to fall apart. To hurt. To disappear. He wept with me so I didn't have to cry on my own with loneliness lurking in my heart and fear stomping me into pieces. Jesus's tears washed away loneliness and fear, exposing my demons and drenching them in love.

Mother Teresa, Princess Diana, and Jesus evicted the fiery creatures clawing inside me and built a home of light and love and lace and grace and sacrifice and purpose and divinity. I was finally touched by God, and the words planted in my mind, watered by his angels, took root and grew. Blossomed into something bigger than myself. I was the Earth and I anchored this beauty in the decay of my body, and I was more alive than my scissors ever made me. I was full. I was whole. I had God. He told me he would keep me safe.

But the prayers and kindness, the words of encouragement, and the phantom caresses I felt gliding across my skin quickly became stilted and stuttering. The voices that once cooed in my brain and the arms that once hugged my heart tightly started to scream and strangle me. The comfort started corroding, and I ached with tarnish. The discolorations were reflections of my sins, branding me because I couldn't be saved. I wanted God to tell me that my pain was beautiful, and yes, I was broken, but I could be fixed. He would fix me. That my troubles were a test of faith. I thought if I believed hard enough, things would get better. I would be better. The divine light would scare away the dark I lived in. The angels would stay nestled in my skull and I would never be alone. But I got sicker and sicker.

Mother Teresa, Princess Diana, and Jesus threw tantrums in my brain. They hit me with their wizened, gloved, and blood-smeared fists. They started in my head, but invaded the rest of my body with gnashing teeth and vicious kicks. They betrayed me. They were my best friends, my one chance at salvation, and they turned on me. I wasn't empty, I was full of traitors. I wept and screamed into my pillow, trying to raise my voice louder than theirs. But they refused to leave. I had lost. I wasn't worth saving. God tricked me into believing his devils were my friends. If God existed, he was cruel. But I realized that the truth was God didn't exist at all. We are alone with our pain until we die. And hopefully, death would be nothing but fading away, submitting to the darkness, and finally resting. I didn't pray to God anymore. Instead, I prayed that death would find me and cure me with its murder.

They gave me meds - meds that would supposedly save me, but definitely killed God. I wasn't a heavenly vessel. I silenced God and his angels one pill at time. I was fine with the killing. God's massacre. The Depakote Assassin. The Lithium Killer. The Seroquel Slayer. Geodon Genocide. The Latuda Murderer. Abilify the Destroyer. Letting Lamictal burn it all to the ground. The medication soon took over, and the crowded halls of my body were emptied. No voices, no screams, no comfort, no torture. I just had pills and a diagnosis. I knew I was crazy all along, but I had hoped that I was just special. But nothing was louder than the rattling of my pills. I had to let go of my angels, of God, and take pills that left me foggy and fat because I was told they were better for me than putting my faith in dead angels. I didn't believe my psychiatrist, but I had nothing else to believe, so I took them by the handful every night. If there was a God, he was now pinned under a pyramid of psych meds.

Over time, I got better. I am better. Thanks to meds and therapy and the real compassion of friends and family. I don't believe in God anymore. He only reaches out to me when I am sick. He is a product of a bipolar mind that just needs something to cling too; something that will hold you in return so you don't spiral into the darkness; a force that tells you it can fix you until it breaks you beyond repair. Mother Teresa, Princess Diana, and Jesus are just signals saying that ,while this may seem like safety, it's step one of losing your mind. When I think there is a God, I am already in the depths of bipolar possession. There's no heaven, just episodes. There's no hell, just cycling. God is merely a misfiring in my mind. I accept that now, and I take my pills and they do their job. The power to get better is in my hands, not those of God or Mother Theresa or Princess Diana or Jesus. They are just manifestations of madness and nothing more.

Sometimes, I really want to believe in God; to have faith in something - something you can turn to for answers, that tells you that this suffering is part of a greater purpose. But my suffering is not by God's divine design. It's by illness. When a heavenly body calls to me, I know that I'm crazy and that I shouldn't answer, but the addiction to salvation is hard to shake, even though I know that God isn't real and he won't keep me safe. But the truth is, I can take care of myself.

No scissors.
No spirits.
No salvation.

I am strong enough on my own.

do what it takes

700 mg Seroquel
1 mg Klonopin
1200 mg lithium
400 mg Lamictal
2 mg Ativan
I'm basically a blob with bed head,
but at least I'll feel better in a few days.
I am hopeful.
I am always hopeful.
I have to be.

anorexia's eyes

When I was younger, I encouraged anorexia to slink into my eyes. It told me how to see myself, and its vision was honest and fair. I was chubby and my frame was layered in extra skin and fat-girl sludge. This is who I was, and this was how the world saw me, so I followed anorexia's advice and consumed less and less and feverishly dreamed of being thin. I would be loved and high off hollowness, and I had a chance at survival because I would be too transparent to be seen. I could slink and slide wherever I chose and I had control over where I went and who could watch me - who could watch my slender, pinched frame glide quietly across the floor. And I would be hauntingly beautiful with gaunt cheeks, a sunken stomach, raised ribs, and protruding collarbones that screamed *I am starving to be this glamorous.*

But I never got there. I was always fat. Too fat to succeed. Too fat to float from room to room with nothing but sexy dark eyes. I savored and feared the freeing emptiness in my withering stomach that winced and whined because I would not feed it, but I failed. I tried so desperately. I never heard my stomach give its final gasp because, instead, I heard my family cry and I saw concern in their bright eyes because they saw my decay. My pinched frame with gaunt cheeks, a sunken stomach, raised ribs, and protruding collarbones made them see someone who was willing to die to be haunting.

I had been living like this for quite sometime when I realized I could never truly be that seductive skeleton with a smoky voice and smoldering stare who was barely there to touch. I grieved when I discovered that I could never be as thin as I needed to be. But anorexia and I still dreamt of dying the skinniest death, in an open casket with chalk white arms placed delicately at my sides. My collarbones raised dramatically above my chest so you could imagine where my heart lay still under a thin, sheer piece of paper skin. I would be gloriously translucent, lying in my coffin, hair plastered to my dusty forehead, coiled in stiff waves, and pink lips that curved into a mysterious smile because I was thin and dead and no one knew why I did it but I did it anyway. My hips would jut upwards and my pale peach dress would dip in between my hips, where there should be skin and stomach, but I had space to spare. Such elegant empty space. And I would be enviably thin and romantically frail and tragically dead.

But instead, I'm alive.

I am still haunted by whispers that worship the art of starving and the tempting promise of a thinner existence. But this time, I choose to live and rely on my own eyes, even on the days when eating feels like failing.

secretly *hypomanic*

Why must everything be so *painfully* beautiful and full? I can't hold in all of this brimming feeling that gives me purpose and heals my wounds but rips my heart open with the intensity of every single sliver of sensation.

The light, the music, the colors, the love simmering in my soul - everything is so orgasmically and *melancholically* intense. It feels so good, it hurts, and I take in everything, unable to say no to any of these tempting opportunities, to slip my hands into unending softness, or hear tinkling music that reverberates in between my ears, or open eyes wide because everything looks so sharply vivid and refreshing, it cuts your heart wide open.

And you FEEL so hard and it drains you to feel everything like this. With this much joy. With this much commitment. I feel it all and I feel it all over and it is *exhausting* and *haunting* and hypnotic, and I can't say no or filter out little fibers because I gluttonously take it all in, even though it tugs apart the seams of my heart.

A single heart can't hold all of these soft, spherical, smooth, shining, bright, twinkling, chiming, piping, palatable pearls that collect in your chambers, growing in numbers and potency, and you are so happy you cry until they drip volumes from your eager eyes. And even these rivers light you *on fire*.

she says less

Anorexia sits behind my right ear,
whispering seductively addictive thoughts about being perfect and thin.

And when I finally take her aggressive advice and stop eating altogether, I can't quite
explain it, I can't describe it quite right, but the emptier I am, the more alive I feel.

I'm high and wild and I picture my insides, just clean and crinkled organs,
not cluttered, not cramped, not full of sludge that's just waiting to be turned into fat.

I'm not weighed down.
I'm not beholden to meals.
I've conquered the weakness of eating, and I am strong and falling apart.
I'm in control, and breaking in half.
The more I refuse, the closer I am to becoming a successful skinny girl.

And even though I'm in agony, at least I can grit my teeth and grin, saying, "I'm okay,"
all while keeping food out.

Out of my mouth and out of my stomach.

But not out of my mind, because the foreign concept of "eating" won't stop rattling
around in my head since I can't make any sense of it.

Haunted by food and feelings and the loud lies that I'm not human and I can run on pain alone.

And that this won't catch up with me.
Eating is just so alien.

It's just easier to exist when I'm empty and about to collapse.

This is all I'll ever be, this is what I deserve.

"You're so lovely as you decompose," she cries into my brain.
"When you're thin and dying and everything beautiful," she screams into my skull.

And the last thing I hear as I faint to the floor is,
"You're better when you're less."

psychiatric secrets; beyond sublime

It's hard hiding delightful sparks of effervescent hypomania when meeting with your overly attentive and intuitive psychiatrist who has never condoned the keeping of psychiatric secrets. Concealing the electric ripples of this illness takes effort and energy, and I'd much rather let it bubble over the top of my mind and course its way through every lightning step I take and every ethereal thing I see and every conductive word I say and every brilliant thought I think. But if my hypomanic tide trickles into the everyday charade of my neurotypical interpretation of "going through the motions," then it will be instantly quelled by MDs and MSWs. It will be taken away. Leaving me painfully estranged from my intoxicatingly mad freedom, and instead stuffed with pills that rattle around in my brain, leaving it completely empty at the end of the day save for the habitual pile up of pill powder debris. Dusty remains taking up much-coveted space that could be filled with awe-evoking brightness and electric fulfillment.

I want to be myself and feel this good, so please just let my hypomania be so I can passionately appreciate everything with a rich depth only I can carry. The wealth of my senses pumping into every piece, part, fiber of my body with a light that ignites such pure divine living and such vibrant visions that all I can do is cry. And feel blessed.

I am a celestial, crazy current. The craziest. Beyond sublime. I never blink.

my fairground

Hypomania is a secret that I can't keep.

Soon enough, it starts to show as I sing too loud and see too bright and feel too much of everything. But until my hypomania is calmed by sleep and just the right pill or two, or a few, I enjoy the swell of love and lust and music and brightness that washes over my entire life.

Everything has *energy* when my manic parade comes to town, strewing confetti and unleashing music in the air and happiness in every heart that comes along to see me perform in my very own show.

I am the most brilliant performer that has ever lived. My ideas are lanterns full of colored lights that others can gaze upon with fondness, envy, or awe as they witness my maddening wonder but are reminded that they are only spectators. They are the neurotypical audience invited to my circus and I entertain and scintillate with my sharp wit and a body that oozes sexual energy.

I am at the center. The crowd *tingles* with my infectious joy and my laugh is contagious as I sparkle and spin around the rink, weaving between glistening crystals hanging from the big top that maybe only I can see but they are just, oh, so magnificent.

As I lie in bed with my husband, wrapped in a manic sequined shroud, I feel every piece and part of him as we love together. Every spot on my body *sizzles* with electricity, as each caress and kiss and nuzzle lights me on fire, my sequins glow so brightly you would think they would never dim. His rough skin, his stubbled jaw line, the smooth space below his ear and right above his collarbones, I touch every inch and shudder because nothing has ever felt so unbelievably in color. His brown eyes staring into mine with pink parted perfect lips saying *love you* letters, and everything is slick and warm and I can see the *sparks*.

The tightrope walker on her wire, I can be poised and graceful, but as we start to move and rub and love, I forget my elegance and fall ecstatically and *earnestly* to the net below as I understand how amazing the world is.

To feel like this is everything, and love is all we are about. Like a Lipizzan Princess balancing on ballerina shoes, holding a parasol, I am such a soft and supple vision. She smiles for the crowds and I can't help but smile for me as I feel so completely *lovely* and *alluring. Why would I ever doubt my beauty?* I wonder, but quickly forget so I can live and love and feel it all *right now* without being marred by the doubts of a me that doesn't have to exist.

And I love my husband as we fuck and *razzle dazzle* the crowd because everyone wonders, *How could they be so in love and so lucky and oh-so-passionate as they wrap themselves around each other?* And they see fireworks that *burst* from our bodies because feeling that sensational is a celebration of every sort.

Ring Master and Bally Girl.

Behold our spectacle as we will—*for one night only* –

(until the Seroquel subdues our act)

love each other majestically and magically under the big top,

because the show must go on

while the hypomania gives us the courage to free fall from the trapeze.

But we never, ever, hit the ground, because there is too much enchanting whimsy in this world.

At least for now.

in tow

My husband clicks computer keys and it sounds like rain.
His words are a heavy storm.
His breathing is like the wind,
steady in, steady out.
My head rests on his heart,
gentle beating, slow and echoed,
clicking and clicking,
raining and raining,
his body is a boat that drifts me off into the night.
I am safe here in his sea.

so much fun

Sometimes when I'm sick, I look totally fine,
and I'm actually pretty fun.

Because, for me, sickness isn't always about being couch-bound, riddled with the sniffles,
a sore throat, aches and pains, surrounded by tissues and cups of tea.
I'm not bent head first over the toilet, puking up my insides;
no queasy fevers, no cold, clammy hands, no curling into a fetal position.

I'm sick, but here I am
at bars and parties,
grabbing you on the dance floor,
laughing at the top of my lungs,
as if fun was a competition.

I'm out and about, flitting furiously,
making people laugh, chattering exuberantly.
My energy is contagious,
my love for life is infectious.
I'm winning at everything.

But my brain is scrambled beyond submission,
my body shakes and everything is too bright.
My eyeballs bulge out of my kaleidoscope head,
my thoughts are vicious, roaring, rainbow tornadoes,
and I don't even notice.

People call me on my "bullshit."
You're not sick! I just saw a photo of you having the time of your life! Cozy in the crowd, making

lewd gestures, with drinks in each fist, a ridiculous grin on your face.
Busted!

And yes,
I'm alluring and adventurous,
impulsive and addictive.
That's me, in between parties and disorderly people.

But what you don't see is my sanity
swept up in a landslide.
What starts out as charismatic and clever
collides into craziness.
Truthfully, I'm brilliant, bold, and barely there.
Everything is falling apart.
I'm sick and so fucking popular,
I don't even realize it.

The thing is,
hypomania is a socially acceptable shade of madness.
People love a party girl,
the wild child,
extroverted angel,
she who's hungry for more self-destruction and entertainment.
That's me in a nutshell.

Because the illness in me can look like fun and light, spontaneous magic, and fiery nights,
but when I'm in that electric place,
handcuffed with dangerously high voltage,
there's nothing magical, only pathological.
I'm sick as fuck.
I'm not depressed, but I'm just as damaged.
It just looks differently.

It's not all depression and devastation with me,
sorrow and isolation.
It's not all psychosis chaining me to the bed.
It's not all fearing the world that lays beyond my lawn,
paranoia and hopelessness are just pieces of disease.

Hypomania is illness fitting in,
but I will fall apart at any moment,
unexpectedly and catastrophically,
trust me.
And then you'll see that my sickness has two sides.

It's hard to treat an illness made up of contradicting arguments.
It's hard to treat what you can't see,
what you don't understand,
when too much happiness is symptomology,
deceptively joyful,
smiling and dying.
This is my bipolar.
So sick.
SO MUCH FUN.
This is
me.

i cut for me

When I cut *just right,* it feels like adrenaline and sex.

Like sex that hurts so precisely, it frees you with an electric jolt of red release and lifts your burdens by ripping you raw. It singes with each inhale. Swollen, sore, tingling. Seductive pulsing, painful pleasure. Gasping red rivers - it feels so good to **ache this way.** My body is ready to brim and break with rushing waves of lustful pain. Please pierce me until I see it puddle through my hungry, straining-to-stay-open lids.

I plead to stay lost in the wound and forget the body that fights to bring me back. I want my scissors to stay stuck in my skin so I can ignore that I exist as an everyday body, chock-full of feelings and memories that make me fat and heavy. Replace with seething sensations, bruised thighs, red on the mattress, angry and full of awe.

Forceful punctures, I am on the cusp of too much. And I don't care. Slit skin revealing the red elation I can make. Sometimes too red, sometimes not enough when my carefully carved cut closes too soon.

I taste my own metallic excitement, and the shock of it all is so decadent and obscene and overwhelming, it makes me sigh with ecstatic surprise and bite my lip thirsty for softness and salt. It is an all too perfect pain that winks a sultry nod as I design yet another erotic slash that promises to drip just for me. I lay **beautiful, powerful,** and **bleeding.** If I masturbate *just right,* it feels like seams snapping apart and it smells like blood and I see my own heavy breath exhaling in an insatiable hurry. Racing against the clots.

I no longer self-harm.

But there are times that I can't help but think about and crave the clarity that comes with cutting so deeply your soul has no choice but to spark.

Nothing wakes you quite like the miracle of making yourself bleed.

The awe from the incision.

The discipline of s l o w l y pulling skin apart - like peeling paper off a present - which, with too much reckless excitement, threatens to leave you exposed.

I can't deny my appetite for earning yet another slice of secret.

But I resist.

It's the right thing to do.

the weirdest thing

The weirdest thing about me is the way my body hates my brain,
and to be absolutely honest, the way my brain feels the same.

Because my body is growing bigger, and while size shouldn't equal shame,
the three-pound pile of goo inside my head says my worthlessness is to blame.

My body hates my brain's sighs, moans, and groans, and the way it always complains,
telling my body that my belly, thighs, and cellulite are wrinkled, pimpled, dimpled terrain.

But despite the threats and bullying, my body won't be tamed.
It's two-hundred pounds of dense and stubborn meat, tacked on a tired, tangled frame.

My brain riots, roars, kicks, and spits a pink pile of pus that's raw and inflamed,
because my body won't listen, won't get smaller - being fat and useless is its aim.

So I have a body seething at a brain because it won't stop calling it names,
and I have a brain that hates a body because of the chubby monster it became.

And the weirdest thing about me is that this fat shaming is a feud I entertain.
I let my brain and body bicker, fight, and argue, and throw my self-esteem down the drain.

Because, though they hate each other, stuck in a relationship that's more than strained,
ultimately, I'm the one who has to deal with both of them while trying to stay sane.

But with all of this constant agitation, anxiety, and doubt, it's fucking hard to maintain.
I feel stuck inside a heavy body that's topped off with an angry brain in chains.

I wonder if I'll ever be free, dethrone them from their reign.
I wonder if I'm losing you because this is a pretty weird problem to explain.

I'm alone and I'm abandoned, I'm just an argument wrapped in skin and tied with veins.
My existence is nothing more than the back and forth of body versus brain disdain.

I guess the truth is I'm completely weird - in fact, I'd say I'm quite deranged,
because after thirty-three years with my brain and body, none of this seems all that strange.

pause

My dog's eyes look like wet marbles.
She stirs at my feet, sighing as she shifts onto her side,
her belly rises and falls, her ears tremble with soft echoes.
Her teeth are sturdy and sharp, she smiles up at me with a grin full of placid fangs.
Her legs stiffen with a stretch right before she tucks them under her chin.
She pushes her wet nose into my palm and tells me
it's time to slow down.

my brain, my body, my weed

I love weed.

I love weed because it makes my mac and cheese taste better.

I love weed because it helps me relax. After a long day of involuntarily tensing and tightening my muscles, it helps me finally catch my breath; to find all of the tight spots in my body and breath into them, slowing my body down, replacing stiff anxiety with a fluid sense of ease.

I love weed because it makes *The Birdcage* even funnier. Remember when Albert pierced the toast?

I love weed because it helps me sleep. I smoke before bed and the day floats away. My mind is delightfully porous and I can't hold on to stressful thoughts. I have no choice but to settle into the soft cloud of my high and sigh into my sheets.

I love weed because it makes me feel cool, like I could totally hang out with the girls of Broad City and the guys of Workaholics. Hazy and quirky and starstruck.

I love weed because it reintroduces me to my body, reminding me that I am more pleasure than I am pain. That I am both gentle and generous. That I don't have to be weighed down by worry. My body is light and warm and I'll be okay.

I love weed because it reminds me of wonderfully blurry college nights when I made an equal mix of good and bad decisions. I inhale deeply and thank God that I've embraced the confidence and security of my thirties.

kallem whitman | 35

I love weed because I prefer smoking than taking Ativan or Klonopin - drugs I've reluctantly been on for years. The fact that I can take fewer prescription medications because something natural can do the job - and do it better - feels liberating.

I love weed because the sensation as the smoke curls in my lungs, and the ritual of smoking out of my window every night, gives me a sense of comfort and control. There's relaxation in the routine.

I love weed because when I smoke I don't have nightmares. I don't wake up, chest tight and in a panic because I feel his hands holding me down. I don't toss and turn, trying to escape a memory. I'm not immobilized by fear, drowning and unable to scream "stop." I love weed because it gives me actual sleep, not five hours of flashbacks.

I love weed because...

It's fun.

It's a sleep aid.

It's medicinal.

It's relaxing.

It helps me manage my PTSD.

I love weed because I'm finally able to listen to what my brain and body need, to curate my self-care, and get back bits of my life.

I'm a white woman, which inherently means I have privilege, power, and access to resources. The fact that I am eligible for medical marijuana and that I can legally possess it and use it is reflective of the institutional and structural racism that permeates every aspect of American life. There are individuals of color who are serving unjust prison sentences for the amount of medical marijuana that I can procure legally. This is an important conversation because we need to examine and challenge how we define justice, understand and unpack the expectations and acceptance we reserve for certain types of people, and fight for equality and equity in all things, especially by dismantling the prison industrial complex.

For more information, please check out The Sentencing Project:
https://www.sentencingproject.org/

unsolicited
advice

Hi young Rachel!

It's me, older Rachel, ya know, from the future. First off, to put your mind at ease, we *do* age well. In the future, it becomes cool to eat lots of cheese and wear leggings. So, don't worry, we've totally got this.

Anyway, the main reason I'm writing this letter is because I want to help you navigate the world with more confidence and better hair. I decided to throw together a quick list of lessons learned and I'm hoping that this information will be both reassuring and will help you avoid some pitfalls. Knowing you, I'm pretty sure you will not take any of this advice - like when mom told you not to take that ice-skating elective in college because you'd break your leg but you did anyway and you snapped your tibia on the first day - but it's worth a shot. Here goes it -

1. Fitting into Abercrombie and Fitch jeans is not an accomplishment! Don't crave sameness. Love yourself as you are. Focus more on being brave than being "beautiful."

2. You actually like sushi! Don't waste time thinking you hate it without even trying it.

3. In your teenage years, you'll start battling anorexia and bipolar disorder and, as you can imagine, these illnesses will threaten to tear you apart. And sometimes, they will. These illnesses are incurable and cyclical, so you will have to manage them your entire life, but over time, you learn how to own your illnesses and you reclaim your identity from these disorders. Please note that this process is expedited when you A) stop doing drugs, B) start sleeping, and C) take your medications as prescribed. Remember, success doesn't mean you will be symptom-free.

4. When it comes to trauma, just know that it wasn't your fault. It was never your fault. I know it is hard, but please believe that.

5. If you want to get tattoos, save your money so you can find a decent artist! You learn

this in your late twenties, but not before getting an early 2000s-style tribal sun tramp stamp. Just because the woman who runs the shop is gorgeous doesn't mean you should get new tattoos as an excuse to talk to her!

6. On a related note, sexuality is often confusing. Invest more time in learning how to genuinely talk to potential romantic partners.

7. On a related-related note, bisexuality is a thing! You don't have to justify your sexual identity. Just go for it, tiger!

8. Bangs are a bad idea. Whether they are trendy or not, bangs are a terrible idea. You just don't have a face for bangs, and that is perfectly okay.

9. You are allergic to coconut. Stop pretending you're not and stop tempting fate. Put down the Samoas.

10. "Fat" is not a feeling. You are taught that being fat means you should feel ashamed, but it is okay to take up space. Being healthy does not necessarily mean being thin. Remember, you need to prioritize both your physical health and emotional health. Hating your body and dangerous dieting will trigger your eating disorder, and you are worth more than being consumed by this disease.

11. Be proud of who you are and what you accomplish. Take credit for your achievements. Just wait and see, you're gonna be a doctor.

12. Therapy and lots of it. It's the best way to find yourself. And you will find that you are fucking fabulous.

13. Watch out! In the future, people will try to trick you into thinking kale is amazing. It is gross. Avoid it at all costs.

14. Be kind to yourself. Always. We all make mistakes. It's how we grow.

15. Give up all hobbies that involve wheels and/or blades. You are clumsy and top heavy and that is perfectly okay.

> With love,
> Older, wiser, and sporting much better tattoos, Rachel

P.S. I almost forgot, this is exciting! In the future, people start subscribing to this liberating concept called "body positivity," which results in a lot of wonderful societal attitudinal shifts regarding bodies, beauty, and autonomy - including the realizations that anyone can pull off a crop top and shaving your legs is optional! See, things do get better.

P.P.S. Don't limit yourself to just eating string cheese. You have a refined palate when it comes to dairy and there's lots of cheese out there!

dream big

I want to become a rapper who addresses real topics for women in their thirties. Following LPs:

- "Pounding the Pepto"

- "Everything Hurts, Esp My Lower Back"

- "Wow, I Like Tea Now"

- "Anti-Patriarchy and Probiotics"

- "Technically, All My Underwear Could be Considered Period Underwear"

- "Am I Body Positive or Have I Just Stopped Caring?"

- "Comfortable Sex Makes the Most Sense"
  (but in a few states, it might be released under the title "Missionary for Missionary")

I think I'd have a solid fan base. My stage name would be Spanxton Hughes.

just a part

A significant part of my identity is being funny, smart, and articulate. The ability to communicate in person and on paper are skills I pride myself in. So, when my medications slow down my ability to process and my bipolar brain suffocates my speech, it's really embarrassing. Honestly, I carry so much shame when this aspect of my illness flares up. When I struggle to find the right words. When I forget what certain words mean. When I can't keep up in a conversation. When I try to write and all I can come up with is neural fuzz. When I have to read things multiple times to come away with anything meaningful. And don't even ask me about punctuation because plopping in a period or a comma correctly feels impossible. It's so demoralizing.

My capacity for plausible sanity is pretty well developed. I can pass as neurotypical, or at least non-symptomatic most of the time, and while maybe these cognitive hiccups aren't super noticeable to everyone else, they are overwhelming to me. They feel inescapable and like little red flags indicating to everyone that I'm crazy. I'm learning how to be kind to myself when I can't hold on to a sentence, when I try to tell a story and keep forgetting what I'm talking about, when I'm typing a blog post and it takes a l-o-o-o-o-ng time to figure out what I'm trying to say and even l-o-o-o-o-o-nger to know how to say it. I'm practicing patience and teaching myself that it's okay to make mistakes, but it's exhausting work.

I need to remind myself that I'm worth it.

I need to remind myself that this isn't who I am, it's just a part of my bipolar.

I am funny, smart, and have a way with words, but right now, things are hard.

But I'll get better.

TWO

mania

moonlit mania

 with the brightest of lights.

Radiating from my shining moonlit eyes, tumbling, twinkling, starlight sparking from my parted lips, fingertips that glow and pulse, footsteps kicking spheres of sunshine across my streets, my ears hear the lightest, loveliest music and the loudest, brilliant illuminations.

Engulfed

Overwhelming love that emanates from this cherished light I hold in my chest; that pours out of this tiny, insignificant person I pretend to be, but truly, I am nothing but stars and moons and suns colliding in a young woman vessel. I beam and brim and seem like everyone else, but I truly shine with the gift of light that others will never know. It crawls deep inside me and nestles in every organ, and if you cut me open, I will bleed firelight.

Enflamed

I beam so brightly for you

until I set my brain on fire.

detonation

Today, my therapist talked about trauma.

They finally figured out that it's not just a matter of fight or flight.
It's not that black and white. It's not one or the other. It's not that simple.

There are more than two ways to try to survive. If you are under attack first, you fight,
next, you flee, and if you can't scratch and kick and bite your way out,
if you can't run and crawl and drag your way out, you freeze.

I started freezing when I was a kid.

It became second nature.

I couldn't fight him off and I couldn't run away.
He was bigger and stronger and made all the decisions. I was pinned by his hands.
I was wedged under his body. I was anchored by his angry words.

To survive meant to freeze.

To freeze my eyes and my insides, my face and my limbs,
to freeze my brain and my body, so I was too cold to feel a thing.

Existing meant freezing.

It meant dissociating.

Protecting a little body that couldn't break free by freezing her into little pieces.
Vacant and expressionless. Little girl icicles stay cold, slick, solid. Stuck.

Until you get older. Then you start melting.

You turn from ice to fire and the puddle on the floor bursts into bright light.

Because I'm thawing out.

I'm too angry to stay cold, slick, solid. To stay stuck.

I'm erupting into flames and fireworks and blistering brilliance.

I am scorching these memories and standing tall under the scalding
blaze that I'm building. I am fierce in my furnace.

Freezing was survival when the world got too painful and the people in it got too violent.
When my body was under attack, all I could be was a girl chiseled from ice.

But now—now, I'm nothing but furious sunlight and broiling moonbeams
and sparking stars burning holes into the sky.

I'm made of raging flames and pulsing heat and my eyes are white-hot and fearless.

My insides are molten, my face and limbs are alive like wildfire,
and my brain and my body are too hot to touch.

Unless you have my permission.

Because I am in control and I make the decisions.

I'm living and burning.

sick and beautiful

The sun sits cradled in my skull, sparkling between two crisp, clean, light-filled eyes. It warms the bridge of my nose and pushes white light through my nostrils. I can breathe in the shimmering scent of space.

My face is soft and open, fleshy mesh that allows the light to pass in and out through my pale pink skin. My freckles transform into pockets of glowing starlight. My radiant eyes are blossoming portals, kindled from my own lavish sun, bridging my being to wherever the light still reaches.

My sun settles warmly, toasting the corners of my mind. My ideas bask in this celestial glow. They ripen as my sun continues to twinkle. These cognitions come out clear and golden and a bit too hot to touch for anyone except me. I can grab each sinewy idea, each delicate strand of genius, and even though it melts away my fingerprints, I don't mind. Surrounded by a wispy galaxy crafted from my own consciousness, with stars and planets I've brought to life, with orbits I keep edging into cosmic motion, I twirl my light into the blackness of nothing that weighs heavy on the edges of time, waiting to overpower the brightness.

I tirelessly stir the sky.

I weave my own stars and my own thoughts tightly into the fabric of blackness that haunts the end of the universe, and even though it dulls my own brilliance, the dispersal of my light into the void makes it smolder with the promising light of stubborn embers. The fire of hope sparks softly.

And while I no longer shine as brightly, at least we can see farther into the night.

the beautiful echo of everything

All music is mine.

I feel it in my fingertips as I flick rhythms forward into cascading shooting stars that pierce our crystal sky...

Lyrics encircle me like twinkling lights wrapped around my reverberating skin as I sparkle and radiate this beautiful sound. It echoes in my too-full heart and I *ecstatically* accept the delicate b.e.a.t.s and the louder laughing orchestra of everything that makes us dance.

My eyes are o p e n,

witnessing the harmony of music, light, color, and feeling—feelings so strong I can see them. My eyes catch glimpses of shooting stars that sing whimsically and sweetly. My eardrums buzz rhythmically alongside the piping of pulsing light bulbs that sparkle as loudly as my never-ending orchestra.

And suddenly, I'm sipping, savoring, swallowing feelings that are so strong and palpable that I can almost touch them with fluttering fingertips, hold them with a heart that is eternally open for more, and celebrate them with a body constantly trying to dance in a world that isn't always throwing a party.

But it should.

Because this world feels so completely and utterly serene and loud and loving, and she is so passionately loyal and so brilliantly honest about her raucous choruses that we should all *surrender* and revel in her noise. This world inspires such sizzzzling, electric music, which makes me truly believe my cascading sky will laugh with light-filled lungs f o r e v e r.

This beautiful echo of everything. I feel it with EVERYTHING that is *mine*.

when *mania rages*

ROAR
I am ANGRY
I feel like ripping my own arms off

And now I am even ANGRIER because if I managed to rip off one arm,
I would be stuck lopsidedly with the other

How can I rip off the remaining limb when one side of me
is already a wrathful, useless gash

I am fucking FURIOUS

Because, to finish the job, I will have to ask someone else
to rip my right twitching limb completely from my body

And knowing my husband, he will try to talk me out of my incensed surgery,
saying it is unnecessary, and that will make me even more ENRAGED

I have my manic reasons, but no one will listen, everyone will care,
and I just want to SCREAM until I'm left with symmetrical bloody stumps

I am INFLAMED
Leave me to my wounds and fumes
I am cursed with dangling limbs I can't get rid of
I am AGITATED and ablaze

I GROWL rabidly into the night

I am absolutely vicious, struggling unsuccessfully in this skin

BOILING in my broken brain
Mania makes me RAGE
All I can do is SHRIEK and SEETHE,
try to wait out the violence,

until I'm too depressed to even lift a finger

exquisitely doomed

When I'm self-indulgently manic, it's like I'm plummeting down a well with glittery broken wings, falling *faster* and *faster*.

As I dive, my heartbeat pulses with exhilaration, my sparkling thoughts are hypnotically destructive, and as I bang my head on each rock jutting out from every which way, as I sink *quicker* and *quicker* into the black brilliance, I just laugh to myself, babble, and conclude that, with every crack of my skull on concrete, I can see brighter, think clearer, and all around transform into

my fucking fantastic true self,

until I hit the ground with a deafening crash and a cringing thud that everyone else seems to hear but me—and there I am, flat on the floor, my ears *ringing* until there's absolutely nothing, my eyes glassy, cracked, and *leaking* rainbows, and all I do is die with a smile on my bloody lips.

Breathtaking.

do your part

My meds have been upped, and more have been added to my nightly say-goodbye-to-the-day routine,

but I still can't sleep.

I lie awake until my eyes burn and the dusty drool pooling on my pillow isn't from soft, sweet snoozing but rather addled, exhausted delirium.

I can feel them bulging my throat, strangling my vocal chords.
My meds stacked in my esophagus.
I'm a human prescription bottle.

I worry that lying down might result in tablets and capsules and pills rolling out of my painfully dry mouth. I'm too tired to try and catch them with my teeth, like a game of Hungry Hungry Hippos. In this scenario, I'm the hippo, angling to gobble up antipsychotics, but I've never had a competitive streak. I wonder if that will do me in.

I'm just waiting for crazy to catch up with me.
I can feel it with each twitch and every blink when there's no sleep on the other side.
I can sense it stalking my every waking step.

I start to power down, from a person to 185 pounds of walking meat stuffed with ten pounds of pills - I'm on so many fucking prescriptions that my heartburn stems from too many meds lodged in my chest and I burp take-800-mgs-at-bedtime dust.

Insomnia is a vicious disease clawing at the corners of my mind.
I can feel myself starting to fray at the seams,

because nothing seems to help me close my eyes and dream of being sane and well rested some day. I lie in my bed, fitful and exhausted, medicated just enough that I can't toss and turn but not medicated enough to slide into a seventeen-pills-does-the-trick restful coma.

This just doesn't feel fair.

And I cry to my husband because I'm doing everything right, but I'm on the cusp of crazy anyway. I'm either going to succumb to depression's quicksand hands or embrace mania with open arms. I'm falling apart at the poles.

And it feels like no matter how long I wait, with my mouth wide open, my head tilted upward like a baby bird impatiently chirping to funnel more meds into my stomach, I'm just going to lose my mind no matter what.

It's not even my mind anymore. It's a waiting room for craziness.
Everyone tells me it's going to be okay, but I'm too tired to listen.
When will this be over?

When will
Lithium-Seroquel-Lamictal-Trazadone-Klonopin-Ativan-Metformin-Risperdal
give me the life they promised?

middle school was *hard,* talking windows made it *crazy*

"Nobody understands the window like me."

The first time I was legitimately crazy in public was in my friend's finished basement. We were sitting in her mom's office, on the worn carpet, looking up at a tiny screen window that was steadily breathing. They were smoking and I was chattering. My mind was rattling, but not from adolescent giddiness or a feeble contact high, just from being crazy. I was in middle school and I knew how I felt wasn't right - it wasn't okay to be this way - but at least it had always been contained before. My loud mind was kept quiet in the silence of my own bedroom. Before, whenever I felt this lost, I would be anchored in my house, and even though my thoughts drifted and shook my skull, I was a well kept secret on the second floor, in the right corner bedroom. I would sit in my own room, somewhat comforted by my own strange security measures, in an average-sized suburban middle-schooler bedroom, flanked by books and stuffed animals. A room complete with a closet crammed with neon clothing, a perpetually disheveled trundle bed, and everything, including me, encircled by a strong firm wall, coated with a healthy layer of light blue paint and dotted with leftover elementary-schooler star stickers. And I would feel weird and alone and scared and like I was being watched, and I would do odd things that didn't make sense but I felt compelled to do them anyway. Over and over again. Like writing poems that at first sounded logical and complete but after reading them a few days later left me feeling embarrassed. Or crying about colors that felt too sharp and unleashed bristled sensations in my scalp that didn't belong behind my tangled bangs. Or cutting into parts of my pink skin with phantom fingers clutching real scissors, just begging my brain to bring myself back into my body - something only pain and blood could do apparently. At least I was inside.

But this time, I sat encircled by friends, next to an old wooden desk, head resting on a broken printer, smelling smoke and hearing laughter, and I looked out that window and it breathed and heaved, and I felt my skin turn into hot sandpaper and my mouth felt empty under my tongue. My words fell to the floor and ricocheted around the room and they skidded across the old beige carpet because they were light and hollow and I was an intruder who didn't belong. Nothing stuck. The window looked at me and sighed and furrowed and I knew it wasn't alive but I understood what she was saying to a crazy outsider like me as she told me to leave. And I didn't hear words, but I knew that it was true as the window caught all our light and filtered the cheap air and pulled out our smoke and she looked down upon me with a glint and a glimmer and a gust that said, "Everyone watches you." That was the first time I was crazy around people, when my madness first started to show, but who knows if they knew or even noticed. They were high and I was staring out a basement window, whispering silently into a tattered screen, pleading with it not to reveal who I really was. And they all thought I must be really fucking stoned, but I was really just fucking crazy, and the window saw it all as she winked down at me and sifted through my secrets, but promised not to tell if I didn't. I needed to keep my crazy quiet and hold it hostage inside my brain, in a body that drifted and came back with cuts that were reserved for places covered by neon clothing. Lock that craziness in your room on the second story of the house you grew up in on the street where you felt so many things. The window said, "I'll keep your secret if you keep hiding," and I felt thankful in my charade. This contract made me safe and unseen. And I winked and said loudly,

"Nobody understands the window like me."

And my friends all laughed because they thought I was high, and I infuriatingly flushed embarrassing shades of red because my secret had escaped so easily from me all at once.

sparkly
rockstar garbage

Being sick and bipolar is soooooomething else.

I haven't been able to sleep well for the past few nights.

Aches and pains, being too hot or too cold, my brain just wouldn't stop buzzing.

Less sleep means I'm precariously close to catapulting my
self-proclaimed "icky" status into being full-blown "sick as fuck."

I also haven't been able to eat much.

My stomach is upset, in part, because I am thirty-two, a neurotic Jew, an IBS fan girl, I live in a perpetual state of food hypersensitivity, and with overactive control issues courtesy of a history of anorexia, and like I said, now I'm feeling "icky" on top of it all.

And since "icky" means I don't eat much,
this also means I can't take my psych medications.

I technically could, but when you have nothing in your system, no mushed up food and bile chillaxing in your stomach and slowly sliding into your lower intestine, it is typically a bad idea to pop a fistful of pills. Because these unapologetically potent bull-dozing psychiatric meds who do their job by pummeling your brain into submission with their very necessary take-no-prisoners brute force can RIP (rip in half, not "rest in peace," however, now that I think of it, both kind of apply) right through your stomach with the same ferocity as they pound the crazy out of your skull. If you have nothing in your belly to buffer the brunt, you feel your insides get hammered. A psych med induced pulverized GI tract on top of the flu? Fucking cruel.

To sum it all up, I'm not taking my meds reliably because I'm not able to eat consistently, and the only thing guaranteed is that I'm struggling to sleep at night. That and I'm getting sicker and sicker and the crazy is kicking in. Now the flu and the bipolar are racing to take over—may the best disease win.

Or may they work together? Disorder meet virus.
What damage can you two inflict as a team?

Being sick and bipolar is soooooomething else.

Now, I am officially "sick as fuck," and my whole body is being mercilessly crushed by the flu. I'm feverish, pitifully covered in two blankets and wrapped in a bathrobe, then everything is abandoned in seconds when I get flushed and overwhelmed by anxiety and hot flashes.

I've got water and Gatorade by my side, applesauce and crackers—it would help if I could stomach something real and take a few Seroquel or at least crunch some Klonopin.

But I can't yet, and my brain starts to rattle and shine. My husband is climbing our wooden stairs to bring me some tea, and he can see my brain glinting and gleaming through the floorboards.

I'm sick and I feel physically awful - like a bag of hot trash that was hit by a truck - but I can't stop smiling. I can't stop smiling and sighing because I feel physically awful - like violent garbage decimated under tire tracks - but my bipolar is wrapping my brain in a delicate condom of doilies with pearl accents.

I'm sick with the flu, but I'm sparkly, and my body hurts and I feel weird, for sure, and my brain is on fire with fever, maybe, but also colorful lights and electric bolts that keep me shivering for more.

The flu tries to mind-fuck me and bring me down, but the bipolar cradles my cranium with starlight and ivory fangs, and I feel sick and disgusting, like sparkly rockstar garbage, and I love feeling my brain sizzle with such radiant fervor.

I'm in bed, sweating through the sheets, and thinking about how brilliant I am, and I can't stop laughing with my husband, even though I'm too weak to sit up and I'm sick and I love it because my brain is purring like a cat cozy on a hot stove.

He loves me, and his forehead creases with concern, but he knows that this is part of the package. He gently pushes toast with jam into my hands, and I nibble and giggle, and he emails the doctor, "She can't take all of her meds right now, which should we prioritize?"

Thankfully, it is Sunday night and he doesn't respond. He is off the clock, so I can stay up until 2 a.m. The party continues.

Eventually, I'll need medication and sleep and food, like the weak, and I'll be stripped from all this bipolar shine. I can smell my brain start to singe with good ideas and not enough moisture, and I know soon that the lace and the glitz and the glamour and the sharp teeth protecting my bipolar brain will inevitably be scraped off and I'll have to come back to baseline and be healthy again.

And I will be "healthy" and thankful, but still somewhat wistful, thinking about the bipolar bubbling that scalded the insides of my mouth for the week I grappled with the flu. Because what a sensation it gifted as it kept me tightly wrapped in fuzzy energy, distracting me with sparkles that burn out your eye sockets. Making me feel so magically superior to the disease of my body.

Flu? Fuck you. I was sick and I soared.

Such a weird, addictive disease, leaving me thanking the flu for my madness.

Eating toast and sleeping. Taking medication that quiets and cools off the whistling steam in my skull. I'm less garbage, I'm less sparkle, I'm more human.

And I have mixed feelings.

goodbye letters
to my body

When I die, they will find notes hidden in the crevices of my skin.

Fleshy letters drafted in ink saying that I was brave more times than I was scared.

Hidden confessions authored by guilt—why didn't I love myself more?—nestled in the glorious creases of a half smiling stomach.

Under my eyes will be carved-out soft spaces for love poems; poetry written for all the colors, the bright light, and energy I was blessed to see.

My arms will be stenciled with a never-ending list that details all of the embraces that they were privileged to know. A list dotted with freckles that brought out my boldness and soft follicles, that prickled with every kiss, reminding me how good bits of body can be.

They will have to dig even deeper to uncover the scrolls tucked in my thighs, written on pink flabby trunks that I religiously disliked but which kept me faithfully anchored anyway. Without me ever having to ask.

And these words will spell out a reminder: you can't run from everything.

But unearthing the volumes squirreled away in the vaulted, chipped crawlspace of my mind will be the most exhausting of treasure hunts. If you persist, you will eventually find my heart written in the margins. And all of these salvaged stories will welcome you and murmur to you: you were loved and I was loved.

But these raw and honest love letters will be the hardest to find. Don't stop looking.

Combing through the crumpled papers stuffed inside my skull, you will also find scrawled scribbles and erratically curled consonants and embarrassingly eager vowels and messy odds and ends of words clumped into categories, and the genre may appear to be something like "frantic revelations" or "manic sputterings," but the real message is that *this was **my** body*. And love always lived here. It always lived somewhere in the cubbyholes of this warm, forgiving skin. Especially when I struggled to believe it.

The very last note reads: I was lucky to live here and, in the end, I'm sad to leave this imperfect and beautiful body of mine. I wish I had treated her better, but I will always love her, even when I can't keep her close.

botched colonoscopy: a love story

People get old and fall apart - a simple and honest fact of life. And if they're lucky, they grow old with someone who helps them pick up the pieces as their muscles atrophy, their vision gets blurrier, their organs act up, elasticity becomes a distant memory, and so on. I am pretty lucky. I met my husband when he was thirteen and I was fourteen - don't worry, we weren't betrothed child brides. We just belonged to the same national youth group. While I did go to his junior prom and we chatted via AOL instant messenger (fucking old school, bruh) throughout our senior year of high school, we lost touch during college. We reconnected and rekindled our romance the summer before our senior year, but he went to school in Pittsburgh and I went to school in Charlottesville. However, both the heart and the flesh were willing to give it a shot, so we decided to try dating long distance. Keep in mind, this all took place before FaceTime, Google Hangout, Snapchat, cell phones with quality cameras, sexting... Long distance dating back in the day took a lot of patience, a lot of creativity, and a lot of buffering. All I can say is God bless Skype, the original gangster. Our love was truly a love for the ages.

We've been together since 2006, and there is no doubt in my mind that this man is my soulmate, which is a good thing because we're married and stuck with each other.

My husband and I love, adore, respect, trust, and believe in each other, and I've never met another human being who makes me feel so utterly and completely safe. But as we all know, there is no such thing as a perfect relationship because relationships require people. And a simple and honest fact of life is that people are beautiful, messy, and complicated. But thanks to ten years of prioritizing communication, sleeping on a king-sized mattress, and embracing the simple and honest fact that couple's therapy can save the day, we've sustained a healthy, loving, and functional relationship. You name the obstacle, we've probably conquered it as a team. Moving a cumbersome fifty-inch TV with a fragile glass base that one of you really wants and the other hates without breaking it: nailed it. Patiently reasoning with and eventually convincing your partner during their "addicted to high end luxury purses" phase that Louis Vuitton and Gucci bags are not a sound investment: crushed it. New jobs and career changes, perilous episodes of extreme hangriness, disheartening mountains of student loan debt, coming home to unexpected pets that your partner adopted during PMS: we've survived it all. In my heart, I thought we would always be there for each other. After the events that transpired in October of 2014, I knew with 100% certainty that our love was real and that my husband and I have a sacred bond that can never be broken. October of 2014 will forever be known as the month of the botched colonoscopy. A medical procedure that will live in infamy. The landmark trial and make-or-break moment of our marriage.

A simple and honest fact about me: I'm a self-diagnosed hypochondriac, but my body is equally untrustworthy. I've endured very real, clinically acknowledged ailments like ulcers, kidney infections, and allergic reactions to coconut. I've also obsessed and agonized over the melodramatic manifestations of highly unlikely maladies like seasonal diabetes, recurring bouts of spinal meningitis, and fear spurred by having an appendix that could explode at any time. My husband has held my hand through it all. He is as patient as I am imaginative. So in the summer of 2014, when I started experiencing severe gastrointestinal issues, I diligently booked an appointment with the best gastroenterologist in town, and my husband was waiting room ready in an instant. Did we expect a concrete diagnosis going in? Honestly, who knows, but since bodies are gross - and medical care in this country is a sham - we were told we wouldn't know anything for sure until after waiting three months (the first available appointment) to have a colonoscopy. I was far from thrilled, my husband and I made a lot of poop jokes, and I booked a slot for my sphincter. We had NO idea the misery that was in store.

Flash forward to the day before my colonoscopy when I had to start prepping for the procedure. If you don't know, a proper colonoscopy requires that your colon be devoid of any organic matter—not even a shred of dignity can remain. This requires lots of pre-procedure shitting your brains out induced by drinking Gatorade mixed with a laxative powder. Specifically, you spend at least half a day trying to swallow a cruel amount of tainted Gatorade and wringing out your body on the toilet. Fun! I'm not being sarcastic—that would've been fun in comparison to the hellish terror my husband and I faced. The morning started out fine and relatively uneventful. I sipped my favorite flavor of Gatorade (yellow) mixed with medical nastiness, gagged a bit on the chalky aftertaste, watched Netflix, and whined. A lot of that activity also takes place over a typical weekend. My husband went to work out, and I dedicatedly chugged my heart out because in order for your body to be colonoscopy-ready, you need to drink ALL of the dreaded mixture and successfully shit out your innards by a certain number of hours before the procedure. If you couldn't stomach the entirety of the crap juice cocktail and 100% completely flush out your system, your colon couldn't get its on-screen closeup with your doctor. A firm but fair rule.

I made sure to pace myself accordingly so I could choke down the necessary amount of colon Kool-Aid and crap my brains out right on schedule. But something wasn't right. The colon jungle juice tasted terrible and made my stomach feel like a tortured twisted death knot, but I wasn't running to the bathroom. I felt more and more queasy, and my mouth tasted more and more like ruined memories of middle school soccer practice (I always drank yellow Gatorade), but I just wasn't shitting. Hmmm. My husband returned to the house and hung out with me, reassuring me that everything would be fine, and I just had to wait until it kicked in. I grew increasingly more nauseous, sweaty, lightheaded, and exponentially more miserable. I was still trying to drink all of the colon hope-cleanse as instructed, but my gut-spasms were definitely getting worse. I have never wanted to shit my pants so badly in my entire life. I wanted to evacuate my bowels and feel better. Let me tell ya, I got way more than I bargained for.

It all started unraveling when, suddenly, I went white as ghost and bolted up the stairs. Was the colon cleanser finally powerwashing my insides? Short answer: kind of. But the crappin' wasn't happenin'. Instead, the first wave of projectile shame and humiliation hit me like a fucking tidal wave. I have never thrown up so violently in my life. I thought I was going to pop some blood vessels. I was vomiting so violently that my body was shaking. My puking had no bounds, and I was pretty worried I was dying. Death by up-chucking. Not in the least bit a flattering way to go. Now for some useful backstory: I REALLY hate puking, and while I know the majority of people do, it's not that I just detest puking - I am also tremendously scared of the process. When I throw up, I panic, cry, and beg for mercy from the vomit gods, whom I picture look like Titans perched on porcelain thrones, plagued by uncomfortable cases of IBS. But a simple and honest and unfortunate fact of life is that, at some point in everyone's life, they end up hurling. Disgusting. However, some people aren't as susceptible to the cringeworthy grossness of barfing. My husband is one of them. When I get sick, he's first on deck to hold my hair back and pat my shoulders while

I simultaneously retch and weep. I have a tendency to empathy gag when people puke, so I'm usually pretty useless, but thankfully, my husband has a stomach of steel. He is a keeper. On that fateful day in October, my steely stud of a husband, with the gag discipline of an ancient Buddhist monk, had no idea what he was walking into as he hopped up the steps to our second floor once-a-bathroom, now a torture cell. Rest assured, he witnessed the fireworks of a lifetime, because my husband came upstairs and found me both on the toilet and puking on the floor.

To give you a peek into our nightmare, at some point, I think I blacked out from the sheer volume of debris rocketing out of me and twisting my clammy half-corpse. I was definitely dying. I was turning inside out. My husband was obviously startled, to say the least, but he actually wasn't as concerned about my untimely, unladylike death. Instead, he was wide-eyed and staring at our bathroom floor, which was painted with a thick frothy coating of yellow Gatorade. Later, he told me he was actually kind of impressed. But at that very moment, not only was I wildly pooping and puking, but I was also sobbing just as uncontrollably. This was it. This was the end of me. When it comes to illness, I am dramatic if anything at all, and I begged Spencer to tell my family I loved them dearly and then implored him to leave me in the house, let me die a tormented death on the toilet, and burn the house down for insurance money, leaving my shriveled remains in the second story bathroom. Thankfully, he did none of those things. But he did comfort me, reassure me, and tell me I'd survive. We would get through this. Throughout the entire ordeal, my husband continued to stand by me (from a reasonable distance, of course), tell me jokes, and vigilantly keep me from fainting and cracking my skull on our tile floor. I would've hugged him in gratitude but I was glued to the toilet and spewing. Finally, when the Gatorade torrents subsided and all that was left of me was a severely abused lower intestinal tract and a withered version of myself that had lost the taste for yellow Gatorade for forever, my husband helped clean me up and didn't make fun of me too viciously. I told him we would never be the same after the things we'd seen, and he said the bathmat would never be the same. As usual, he was more right than I was.

I learned a valuable lesson that day. A simple and honest fact of life is when you have a partner who loves you, he won't abandon you at your most gross and then torch your house to get some sweet insurance cash. That, my friends, is love in its purest form. For this is the incredibly unglamorous, unadvertised side of marriage - being there for your partner when things get hard, times get tough, and you are at your most repellent. I could barely handle catching a glimpse of my dried up self in the mirror that evening, but my husband loved the shit out of me—well, he would've if there had been any left. He loved me, he cleaned our bathroom floor, he threw away our bathmat (RIP blue shag), and he rid our house of any evidence that we once had yellow Gatorade (to this day, seeing it triggers

PTSD flashbacks. PTSD being the acronym for Puke Trauma Survivor and Denier). After the incident, I was literally emotionally and physically drained, and also overwhelmingly embarrassed. Because, yes, we have been partners for a decade, but those three or so hours of horror left me at my most vulnerable and fragile. Being that disgusting in front of someone is really tough, utterly undignified, and immensely miserable. But I was right about something: ultimately, as disturbing as the experience was, it actually made us better. We weren't the same. We were a much stronger couple. Because a simple and honest fact of life is that when you find your soulmate, the person you were meant to be with for the rest of your days, you acknowledge and accept that they are beautiful, messy, complicated, and subject to eventually falling apart, but you wouldn't miss a minute of it. The trick is building a relationship in which you can both get old and be gross together with enough love, laughter, and patience that you are not driven to third-degree arson.

Key facts to leave you with:

1. Turns out I had an allergic reaction to the colonoscopy prep materials, which caused this physically and morally disturbing experience.

2. My colonoscopy went fine and my stomach issues are mostly under control now (yay!).

3. My husband and I are still together, still in love, and still gross. It's not that we're proud of being repugnant at times, but rather we both have succumbed to learned helplessness and embrace our inevitable ickiness and mortality.

4. We have four new bathmats!!!

5. It is my husband's turn to be disgusting, and no matter what his body has planned, I will be by his side... but maybe from a reasonable distance.

on repeat

I lie in bed, on my back, above the covers, decked out in my swimsuit. I cradle my iPhone between my shoulder and my ear as I blast M83's "Do It, Try It." I turn the music up and nudge my phone closer and tighter, my clammy neck hugging and holding the phone, positioning it so the speaker blares directly into my ear canal. The music is loud, electric. It erupts in my skull, sparking and sparkling.

I see bursts of white light.

Each and every crescendo is accompanied by the fizzing of fireworks popping across my eyelids. I'm grinding my teeth, but the music is too potent, too powerful, too alluring, too everything. I'm gritting and grinning, and I can't hear my jaw clenching over the sounds of my brain feverishly percolating.

My bright, addled eyes register as half-alive. Unreliable headlights. Switching on and off. A seductive strobe light blinking and winking to the throbbing of electronica. My skull is swelling with the now familiar lyrics – I've been playing this song on repeat for the past forty-five minutes - and the magical madness presses aggressively against my temples. Thumping my hollow bones to the beat. My body and brain are distracted by the music and the warm euphoria blossoming in my chest. Spilling onto the mattress.

I'm blushing and brilliant.

My skin is embarrassingly splotchy, but I'm the most beautiful I've ever been. Inside and out, I'm adorned with twinkle lights, wrapped around my lungs, lassoed around my heart, constricting concentric circles tied taught around my stomach. Candlelight dripping from my lips and fingertips. My phone is wedged further into my ear as I kick and lift my glowing limbs. Paddling my flippers with clumsy grace, I work out my routine.

I'm elegant and drowning with every ragged breath.

I am the captain of the Olympic synchronized swim team and I need to learn every stroke, every flick of the wrist, pair it with flair and flamboyance, and, more importantly, I need to teach my recruits. Soon, I'll have a gaggle of Olympic hopefuls looking to me for guidance. Their saucer-sized eyes following my every twitch, glitch, and reflex, committing it to memory so we can compete as a well-oiled machine with me at the helm. I lie on my teal comforter and tremble my luminous toes, cup my glittering hands, move in tune to the music blasting in my head. I grab my floatation device, once my husband's pillow, and I rest my cheek on its cotton surface before returning to my work.

My labor of love, my craft, my calling.

Oh, to be an Olympic angel, even though I hate swimming. But I focus with red-hot intensity on perfecting each and every aspect of my routine, with my music looped for eternity, my teeth dancing themselves into dust, my muscles eager to learn move after move, my ears vibrating, my fingertips pulsating, my eyes dry and cracking, my lips twitching, capturing a smile, because I am worth the gold medal. I am dedicated and diligent, even as my lights shudder, flicker, and dim because I left the window open.

Keep your eye on the prize, I whisper to the walls.

Kick and twist. Squirm and stroke. I swim and smirk in my black and white polka dot swimsuit and I lean to the side, coming up for air, a quick jerking movement to snatch some tattered oxygen with my porous pearlescent lungs. Everything feels like it's falling into place. It feels simple and perfect. I dunk my head, closing my eyes, my ears waterlogged, and I raise my arms with resolve, I'm ready to lead my team. I point my toes, cloaked in purple socks - or maybe they're fins - and flutter kick them until my ankles ache. I stretch my legs symmetrically. I hold my breath. I'm ready to dive.

To take the plunge. To win.

I slide to the surface, blinking back chlorine, and flaring my nostrils. I'm going for the gold. Even if it means living life submerged. But my husband reaches across the sea for my dry fingertips and slips a Seroquel into my dusty, pale palm. He tells me to come back to dry land. The blankets aren't waves. The piles of pajamas aren't swimming lanes. I turn off my music and peel off my swimsuit. My Olympic dreams dashed. All it ever was, was madness. I'm shattered and confused as the lights snuff out. Losing the purposefulness and bliss I once had.

It's over before it even began. Beached in the expanse of my sheets.

i bleed the universe

My friend got me this pin for my denim jacket. It's an enamel hand, cupped upward, severed just below the wrist. And where flowing blood should be, there's an outpouring of stars and moons and galaxies in its place. On the paper packaging, underneath the gold-plated cosmos, it reads, "I bleed the universe."

This is the most bipolar thing I've ever seen.

Because when I'm in the throes of my illness, lost in the throng of my manic moons and stars, my madness throbbing melodiously against my temples, my eyes watering with the overwhelming wonder of everything I see and sense and know and love, with an echoing heartache that's synced to the pulsing of a thousand galaxies, I truly believe that if I was to unbutton each wrist, peel my skin with precision, twist off my fingertips so the light could shine out, then there would, in fact, be more universe than blood. More moonlit heaven than fiery red hell. More twinkling star shine than rusty orange mud. The blinking lights of the universe pooling in my skinless palms.

I've slit my wrists before, seeking stars and sunshine, digging deep into my veins, searching for something to tell me that I'm special. That I'm not actually crazy, I'm godly. I'm not trying to kill myself, just trying to confirm that I am the one. That everything I do is divine. That I'm practically magical. That I am kin to each and every god that lives above my head and nests in my heart. They smile at me and wring their hands, raising their own severed wrists above their heads, chanting into my deafened ears that I am the key to this existence. Sometimes the words are too tangled to slip from their lips, but on other days it's all I can hear. My mania mouthing madness into my eardrums.

When I'm that crazy, I cup the sky and cry and pray and raise the sunshine above my head as my dark blood trickles down my arms, carving red rivulets in my pale skin. My arms collecting constellations, masquerading as clustered freckles. I'm blessed with blood that gushes from my open hands, splattering my face with divine grace. Coating my smile in dark pink celestial lipstick, leaving my mouth ringed with rosy red sunsets. Anointing my forehead in angry red holy water, eyes dotted with bloody moons. My tears are salty, wet, and crimson, and they say to the world that I am bloodletting and brilliant. The wounds hum and sting and remind me that I am more than alive. I'm magnificent. The pain sets me on fire and I feel freer than I've ever felt before. A shimmering asteroid hurtling through the nothingness of space. The eclipse kisses my forehead and I slide blissfully from bipolar to solar. I'm a shooting star escaping from my dying body. When I'm crazy as fuck, I really do bleed the beautiful universe.

But when my mania turns into darkness - iridescent madness mutating into a psychotic void - the red ripples binding my body crust over and become clusters of black massacres. My mind is muddled with scars and shadows, and my brain misfires until I taste metal under my tongue. I dig into my skin with fevered fingers, and I douse my wounds in salty water, but I can't conjure a goddamn thing. No gods this time, no shine, no purpose, no mercy, nothing. Empty blood and hollow bones. I don't die, but I barely exist. Nothing but a skin-covered graveyard of collapsing stars. My sparkling shroud shatters and glass piles around my feet. Broken halos and moons bent out of shape. I step on a sun and slit my soul. I'm crazy and scared. I'm insane and frightened. I'm bipolar and bursting open. I'm lost in my own weak wrists. I smear the blood from my palms, peering into the pulp, I press my eyes so closely to the incision that they blink back blood, but I never see that sunrise. I can't find the planets. The meteors. The cosmic dust. I just find aching hands that quiver under the cuts. And I cry, hunched on my knees, banging my head methodically against the kitchen floor, asking my skylight why I'm not in orbit as blood clots on the kitchen mat.

Isn't this the most bipolar thing you've ever seen?

my bella fabulous

My dog, Bella Fabulous, doesn't care that I'm crazy. I don't think she even notices. Because for her to take note would mean comparing me to someone else, and I'm pretty sure I'm the only person she cares about.

Bella Fabulous loves me the same when I'm cycling and when I'm not. Sick or healthy, she's always by my side. Laying at my feet, snuggling with me on the couch, sitting watchfully in my lap, kissing my face when it's covered with tears and when it's covered in food, and staying close when I'm confused and frightened of the things that really exist and the things that only exist in my head. As far as Bella's concerned, I'm enough.

I don't know what I would do without my Bella Fabulous - the bringer of comfort, the eater of crumbs, the warmer of feet, the exuberant greeter when I get home from work, the one who looks up at me with unconditional love in her honey brown eyes. I am so thankful for her snaggle-toothed underbite, her coarse brindle fur, her crooked tail, and her floppy ears. I'm even thankful for her farts. She is such a big part of my life. She helps me keep my life on track. I can't imagine what our lives would be like without each other. As far as I'm concerned, Bella Fabulous is my stinky everything.

Bella Fabulous is my doting companion and she gives me purpose. Even in my darkest moments, I know I need to stay here with her because she needs me. She needs me to feed her, to walk her, to love her - something that only I can do. Even just the ritual and expectation of taking care of Bella Fabulous every day is enough to keep me moving, to promise tomorrow, to take one step forward with cheese cube and leash in hand.

This post goes out not just to Bella Fabulous, but to all the pets who make a difference - who make life worth living when you really need a reason to keep going, when you need evidence that existing is your only option. This post goes out to all the pets who love you and rely on you. And to all the owners who know how hard life can be but still take it one belly rub at a time. Life requires a team approach, furry members included.

for love

"How can I be broken when my heart is illuminated with lit candles?" I answer when he asks me. My smile is garish and wide and full of crooked teeth. The blue eyes lodged asymmetrically in my skull glitter and glow, twinkling with conviction. I'm kinetic and vicious.

"There's no answer!" I sing to his stalling.

He pauses because he has to tell me I'm crazy. I'm happy now, but mere moments away from becoming cluttered and clunky, weeping and sinking, frantically clawing my way out of the mental milieu I hate the most. When madness meets depression, rotting raw violent holes in my brain. He lulls and lets his thoughts linger, letting me savor this spinning sensation that sets me on fire.

"Except for love and lipstick." I say out loud, answering a question he didn't ask. Proudly boasting my secret recipes, revealing the saturated shades of the universe, toasting my genius with such brilliant beacons, such pearls of wisdom like, "Loneliness is impenetrable, except for love and lipstick." I laugh too loudly, I smile too aggressively, and pearls and beacons and brilliance and universe bounce from between red-stained gums.

I hug him so hard my own hands shake.

And he looks at me with love and concern and routine, and he kisses my temple - the soft spot on the side of my face that is radiating electric ideas. A bullseye so angry, hot wisps of my hair won't lay still on my skin. He tries to quiet the vibrations that scramble my teeth, and folds his arms around mine, pulling me close, pulling my heart into his chest, holding me too tightly and too softly all at once. And I laugh and I cry a little and, before he even asks me if I have a Risperdal in my pocket, I rattle, "Prepared, like the weatherman packing his rain coat."

To love a crazy woman.   But he never, ever says it like that.

i took body positive boudoir photos and i feel meh

My husband suggested it - that we spring for a boudoir photoshoot, that we get all gussied up and wear lacy, sparkly, stringy things, and curve our backs, and bat sultry, smoky lids, summoning sexy half smiles for the camera. I was reluctant because that shit is expensive and because I am fat.

I haven't been fat my entire life. In fact, I started out as a pretty average-sized kid who just thought she was fat. The war with my body started in middle school, when I lamented over my chubby thighs and doughy stomach. I agonized over rolls of flesh that felt synonymous with failure. There were times when I found it nearly impossible to love myself. But there were also times when my body was my best friend, like when I slide tackled a cocky forward during a soccer game and my thick legs made me feel powerful and brave. When my first boyfriend told me that I was beautiful and built like a woman. When my dad charged me with mowing the lawn because I was more muscular than my thinner, older sister. My relationship with my body was not black and white. It was shades of pasty, fleshy peach.

It wasn't until high school that I started doing serious damage. During my freshman year, I dabbled in "dieting" and, unfortunately, I was really good at it. My unwavering willpower enabled me to forego sweets and "unhealthy" foods (which was actually just code for anything), and I started losing weight. I would grab my stomach throughout the day and I was increasingly impressed every time it felt smaller. I realized that I could eat less and less and rapidly lose more and more. And even though the result - on top of the desired thinness - was debilitating headaches, fainting spells, organs that struggled to keep on trucking, and coming close to dying, at least I wore a size two. But ultimately, no matter how thin I was, how many ribs I could count, how far my collarbones protruded out of my translucent skin, I hated everything about myself. I would never be thin enough, never be good enough. My body betrayed me with every bite I took.

I never thought I'd survive anorexia's grasp. The only consolation was that at least I'd be painfully thin, lying in my practically empty coffin.

But I lived.

My unwavering willpower did a complete 180 because, apparently, I didn't want to die after all. I lived, and my skeletal body began gaining weight. It became easier to think and exist, and life was less physically painful. Emotionally, I oscillated between feeling liberated from disease and feeling weighed down by a body that started growing. A shaky frame soon became solid mass. And despite my dread and panic, my pasty, fleshy peach body kept accumulating more and more pounds - a response to recovering from anorexia and dangerous dieting as well as a product of my decision to finally take my psychiatric medications, all of which listed "weight gain" as a possible side effect, or, in my case, a guaranteed side effect. For the first time in my life, I was really fat - definitively fat - and I couldn't figure out how to feel about the mounds of flesh stretching out my skin because I was also the happiest I'd ever been. I had enough energy to live my life—to get my Master's degree and hold a job. I stopped irritably snapping and scowling at my husband. I could actually sleep at night because I wasn't starving, people were no longer worried that I was about to keel over, and my parents held less concern in their eyes. But I also had to go to specialty stores for larger ladies in order to find clothes that fit. My necklaces with sixteen-inch chains started fitting uncomfortably snug under my chin. I was preoccupied with dread when I went out to eat thinking people were judging what was on my plate and what I shoveled into my mouth. Navigating the world in a fat body, in a fat shaming society, was perilous. I felt ashamed and embarrassed of my size, and often anything but sexy.

But here's the thing: other days, I felt big and beautiful. I read articles on Jezebel and Hello Giggles about embracing body diversity, I watched videos on Buzzfeed starring fat women giving testimonials that fat self-worth exists, and I listened to the gospel of Jessamyn Stanley, Tess Holliday, and Lindy West, all touting the essentiality of body positivity, fat positivity, and challenging fatphobia. My breasts went from barely As to triple Ds, my thighs were strong and sturdy, and I felt curvaceous and luscious. There were periods where my body was not just a means to move through life, but my beautiful, fat vessel. Two-hundred pounds worth celebrating. But at the same time, there were periods where I felt disgusted by my ugly, fat frame. I was tangled in this perpetual back and forth conversation with my body about my body.

A few months ago, my husband and I read a few articles about how empowering boudoir shoots could be. I watched the documentary *Embrace*, which explores body positivity by interviewing women all over the world and it features a segment on how photoshoots can boost self-esteem by showing you the real you - the beautiful you that other people see. Soon enough, I allowed myself to become intrigued and decided that a boudoir shoot had the potential to help me make some peace. We booked the shoot and showed up with lingerie in tow and sheepish smiles. I was nervous, especially because getting into the studio required trudging up a steep flight of stairs that left me unattractively panting, but I had a sun-shiny *let's-get-this-over-with* attitude. My goal was to keep my belly as covered as possible, part and pout my lips, and plump up my cleavage. My husband stood much more confidently in his black boxer briefs and the leather jacket we got him in Paris. Lights, camera, action.

I felt shy and sexy. I felt fat in a bad way, I felt fat in a good way. My hair and makeup made me feel seductively put together, my nipples were delightfully pointed, the dimples on my thighs were suggestive, and the way I arched my back made my butt look perfectly pert and my breasts look deliciously perky. As I got more comfortable during the photoshoot, more clothes came off and there was more laughter. My husband and I both beamed as we posed around the studio, from caressing on satin sheets to curling together on furry rugs. Despite all the hairspray and being mindful of my stomach, it did feel freeing. Afterwards, as we walked back to the car, my husband still bouncy and my fake eyelashes still glued in place, I felt like the most desirable woman in the world—well, at least in Pittsburgh. Still riding the post erotic photoshoot high, my husband and I went out to dinner at a fancy restaurant so we could take our sexual magnetism on a date. I felt phenomenal.

But a few days later, feelings of insecurity resurfaced. It dawned on me that I had just taken a slew of photos of me prancing around in a larger-than-average body. My chubbiness saved for posterity's sake. Maybe it was stunning chubbiness, but I began feeling more and more bleh. And the bleh culminated, coming to a head when the time came to check out our photos. Two weeks after the shoot, in the studio where it had all gone down, we sat with the photographer in front of a large TV monitor where our photos were thrown up for our viewing pleasure. Now was the time to pick the photos we liked, the ones worth paying for. My husband and I sat in front of our slide show, critiquing the photos - and thus, our bodies - and at times, this felt incredibly uncomfortable, like when a photo caught my body at a bad angle, but other times, my soft skin and bright red lipstick made me smile. We sat there for an hour or two, scrolling through photos and feelings. After plunking down our credit card, we pocketed a USB key with twenty-five photos saved on it, and I padded down the steep staircase, caught between feeling like a proud, fat feminist and feeling like I never wanted to tell anyone about my fatness caught on film.

And here's the thing, a month or so later, and I still feel this way. I just whipped out the USB key and started clicking through the images, and there are some in which my body looks amazing. And there are others that make me blush from embarrassment because you can see too much of everything—and I have a lot of everything. But I see the photos for what they really are: just moments captured in time. Images connected to feelings that come with a lifetime of living in this body.

When it comes to understanding my body, I've learned that it is okay to vol-
ley back and forth between self-love and self-loathing. This ongoing conversation doesn't
make me a terrible feminist. It's normal, to be expected in our heteronormative, patriarchal,
misogynistic society that teaches us we are never enough. This relationship with my body
makes that photoshoot feel both empowering and disheartening. The experience didn't
cure my waffling body image, it didn't change how I forever see my stomach, even with
professional hair and makeup and flattering lighting. The photoshoot didn't enable me to
completely forgive and embrace my fatness. But it did remind me that I do think of myself
as beautiful—maybe not all the time, but there are definitely moments worth capturing.
Loving your body is never a constant. You're always going to have good and bad days. My
advice: just be patient with yourself and enjoy those photos when you can, because that shit
is really expensive.

bipolar love

When I'm manic, I love myself so much it feels like
I might burst into a thousand glittering pieces.
I want to hug myself to death, rub myself to death, push and pull and tug myself to death.
I would be fine dying in my own sparkling arms, except I can't sit still.

My self-esteem is off the charts,
a happiness that is unprecedented,
unparalleled to any emotion that anyone has ever experienced,

ever.

With each brilliant breath, I'm the best there ever was and the best there will ever be.
I'm so perfect, I can't sleep.

It's hard to put into words the surging joy that floods my veins,
this dazzling radiation bleeding into my body,
this divine realization that
everything I do is amazing,
every thought I have is genius,
everything about me is undeniably magnificent,
everyone around me admires me, loves me,
or else eyes me suspiciously because they're jealous,
envious of my non-stop rattled chatter, my cracked shaking hands,
my twirling shimmering thoughts, the light that blinds everyone but me.

Anything is possible.
I'm alive and luminous, energetic and iridescent, bedazzled with sharp edges,
so painfully bright and viciously lovely,

my smile takes up an entire room, my laugh overwhelms the neighborhood,
the city can't keep me under control.
I'm in charge of the future.
Listen and latch on to my glistening plans
because I am always too shiny and right to be regular and wrong.

I always forget how to be lonely and how to feel inadequate.
My doubts dissolve into piercing colors and wild lights,
and the true blessing is that I see the beauty in everything,
especially in myself.
Suddenly, I own an exquisite body,
a body that I usually hate.
My self-loathing mercilessly drowned in insatiable desire.
A body so unapologetically mesmerizing and electrifying that it doesn't need to eat.

I live on embers and bright ideas.
I get my energy from the sun and the moon and the stars
and the freckles playing patterns on my pale skin.
I'm elated and ecstatic and all around exaggerated.
I'm the embodiment of everything extraordinary.
I'm fractured and blissful.
To die in my own fire would be a breathtaking dream.

My mind on mania is everything beautiful, indulgent, and sick,
a love affair that leaves me broken and cursed and dangerously infatuated.
It's hard treating this disease when it feels like it's the best thing about me.

I guess I love bipolar more than I love myself.

kin

I am bipolar and bonkers and irrefutably boring.

I have nothing to offer.

I wish I wrote as eloquently as Virginia Woolf, with beautiful articulations like Sylvia Plath, lying lyrics on old paper that inevitably stained but remained profound and potent like the poems of Dickinson. But I don't have the grace of their inkwell-laced letters or their unparalleled talent for authoring authentic emotion, nor do I live a shadowy life of insane despair with a dash of lesbianism. Well, maybe except for that last bit.

600 mg of Lamictal leaves blue dust in my palm.

All of them so intriguing, these women of my illness. I just don't have their phrases, or their penmanship, or their pedestal-worthy exit strategies, like walking into a river for the sake of peace, or peeking into an oven, looking for something slightly larger than nothing.

But I feel the same, pained cranial chaos. The same shattered rattle in my limp, soggy heart. Eyes that bleed black. And a sickness that stops me wherever I stand.

Two little red Risperdals right after breakfast.

I just don't have the poise or the elegance or the brave nature of my sick sisters from long ago; the founding mothers who chiseled the foundation of our shared madness. They lived their lives in parlors and log cabins, sharing beds and gardens with other tortured creators. They left behind everyday artifacts, museum-worthy antiques, countless possessions that deserved preservation. Trinkets and treasured belongings. Petticoats and typewriters. Old coins and folklore. Everything much more inspired than mine.

A Klonopin to stave off a panic attack, please.

All I have is a faded couch propped up in front of a large television that spills reality TV shows into my living room. I wear ugly pajamas that I bought at Target. For the love of god, TARGET. How unimaginative is fucking Target? I guarantee you no future historian will ever catalogue lyrics and sonnets dedicated to the miraculous muse that is Target. Emily Dickinson would never go there for her bonnets.

But they do have my prescriptions.

My bipolar is not romantic.

Not an illness to share sentimental silence with. I am not a recluse writing poetry on slips of paper to crush into crevices in my father's library. I have a laptop with a perpetually low running battery and Florence and the Machine looped on my iTunes. No pen or paper or pebbled leather notebook, no harpsichord or violin or piano. Nothing classic. Just Flo belting out ballads and me clacking computer keys. No cursive characters or daguerreotypes from days of yore, no quills with inked tips, nothing timeless.

I press a tablet of Zoloft onto my tongue.

I don't use words like "ethereal" or "gossamer" or "pallor" in everyday conversation. I guess I could, but I don't because the words of my generation are "selfie" and "Netflix and chill" and "FOMO" and I use those instead. I am unabashedly all over Instagram. Because I am lazy and predictable. What do I even contribute to feminism? I am a real fucking phony.

My Seroquel keeps getting upped but at least my teeth have stopped shaking.

I hide behind a glowing screen and string together long extravagant paragraphs crammed with adverbs, elaborate whining, and imagery that is ultimately juvenile and hollow. I barely scrape by as I try to be vivid and Plath-like, harkening the depth of Emily and Woolf, but I guess it's insincere because I'm just a disheveled fake—especially considering my modern day madness doesn't even compare to the real throes of desperation that picked off the masterful crazy ladies of history. They made space for genius and I just refuse to shower.

At the end of the day, I am a miserable, monotonous, manic mess.

I chew Lithium as my eyes roll back in my head. But admittedly, it is easier to breathe.

I am such a disappointment when it comes to collecting crazy for posterity's sake.

I groan in the bathroom mirror and dry swallow a combination of tablets and capsules. But at least I slept through the night and my thoughts have stopped whimpering.

Inelegant and obnoxious, I share nothing in common with the mentally ill heroines who kept track of their crazy in stories we salvage. My woeful words and my shoddy lesbianism never held a candle to their legacies. I will leave nothing behind except for my unpaid Target credit card balance and a measly Word document reluctantly titled "ideas."

But two Ativan later and I get my life back.

A big difference between Woolf, Plath, Emily and me
is that I'm not "blessed" with the trope of broken brilliance.

I'm sick, but not doomed. I'm crazy, but not damned.

I'm going to make it.

holding hands
before bed

When nightmares appear, we are within arm's reach,
wrapped up in dreams, love, life, and sheets.

i eat my crazy

Flossing deep into tender red gums, fishing particles
of Lithium from between my jagged teeth.
No more psychiatric morsels tucked up in the attic of my mouth.
I can finally wash away the chalky aftertaste
of Lamictal shavings hoarded at the edge of my throat.
See me scrubbing clean Seroquel's talcum thumbprints that
press into the creases and crevices of my lips, teeth, gums, tongue,
and the insides of my cheeks, so I don't taste the crazy residue.

I'm all better now.

weight for it

Weight for it.

Weight until you lose fifteen pounds.
Weight until those old jeans fit.
Weight until you stick to your diet.
Weight until you exercise every single day.
Weight until you can count your ribs.
Weight until you don't make any mistakes.
Weight until you're so thin that you're perfect.
Weight until people tell you you're beautiful.

Just weight.

Because only then will you be worth it.

I just bought a belt.

And this is significant because I haven't worn a belt in over a decade.

Growing up, there was never a scale in our house, so I would use a belt to determine if I was losing or gaining weight. Every notch had the power to devastate me or elate me. Little holes bored into leather, cut into cloth, that measured my worth.

When anorexia really took over, I begged and begged my mom to buy a scale and, understandably, she refused. In fact, one of my therapists suggested I not have belts because they served as a way for me to obsess and agonize over any fluctuations in my weight.

In college, I got some of my belts back, acquired new ones, and the torture continued. This notch meant I was too fat and unloveable. If I reached this one, I'd be thin and life would be perfect. But no matter how little I ate or how sunken my stomach was, it was never enough. I was never enough.

I moved to Pittsburgh in 2007 and I left my belts at home. I realized that I was more valuable than a dotted line pierced in fabric - that this was a terrible way for me to measure how much I loved or hated myself. But the other day, I walked into GAP because a pair of my pants were too loose. So, I bought a belt. And the only thing that's changed is that now my pants stay put. My love for my body has not, and will not, change. I refuse to quantify myself, to assign a grade or numeric value to my body or my happiness.

I love who I am. And I like the cute belt I just bought.

nothing
left to take

I wonder what I'm going to be like when I can't afford my meds anymore. Hmm.

Because, eventually, health insurance will become even more of a luxury than it already is and only the one percent will be able to afford all the co-pays and treatments and appointments and surgeries and medications - you name it.

Inevitably, I'll run out of money.

I'm married to a cis white man, so I imagine, for a while, he'll be able to negotiate favors. His skin and his sex will give him connections. His master's degree and his Anglo-Saxon, easy to pronounce, non-threatening last name will give him instant access.

He'll talk about "grabbing pussy" in the locker room with pharmaceutical execs just to gain their trust, to be one of the guys, because that's what boys do, and boys will be boys. And he'll probably score some discounted Seroquel. "She's a good fuck when she's not crazy," he'll say to sound convincing.

But let's be honest, how long can that last? Six months max?

Because the cost of medication is going to keep increasing. It's going to sky rocket. Men who aren't doctors make decisions about the vitality of pills. They probably don't care that it's a matter of life and death because, to them, money is what matters. And who are we to think that medicine shouldn't be a business? Medicine is all about stocks. Medicine is about investing.

Medicine is money.

I bet my husband and I will be able to scrape together enough cash for antipsychotics for a stretch of time. More locker room banter will buy us some leeway—a price cut for good ole boys, even those with crazy wives. But yeah. We'll run out of money, we'll lose our insurance, the price of meds will keep going up, and then I'll lose my mind.

I'll do my best to titrate off everything as slowly as possible—parcel out my pills as best I can. The Lithium, the Seroquel, the Lamictal, the Ativan, the Klonopin, the Zoloft, the birth control. Yeah, that last one will be the first to go, which will be a big problem if I get knocked up while I'm on my other meds because I'll be forced to bring a fetus with gills and a face full of glassy eyes into the world.

No abortions, not even for fish children conceived on drugs that seep poison into my womb. I'll have to give birth and then bury it. Closing all its eyelids ceremoniously at its Pence-sponsored funeral. Good night, sweet abomination.

I imagine I'll count out my meds carefully, gingerly putting smaller and smaller piles of pills into my day-of-the-week plastic organizer, breaking them in two so they'll last longer. Savoring the sanity for as long as possible. Bracing myself because I have no choice but to go back to the chaos that is unmedicated bipolar. Coaching myself that *I can do it.* Telling myself it'll be okay, even though I know it won't be.

And then I'll be down to only one or two pills a day. I'll lick my index finger and dutifully trace it across the plastic walls of my prescription bottle. I'll coat my tongue with Lamictal residue as I try to steady my thoughts. Reminding myself I need to focus.

Without my meds, I think crazy thoughts and the world is a crazy place, so I'll vigilantly remind myself to STOP THINKING CRAZY. I'll dig my fingernails into my arm, scolding myself not to be scared. I bet if I bleed I will be braver.

Soon enough, I'll stop sleeping because my ideas will keep me awake. And the voices and the visions. The delusions will do me in. I'd bet money on it. And even though I might be manic for a while—I might see this brilliant beauty radiating out of a broken existence, telling everyone that there is light and hope and divinity, *I see it, I feel it*—I will be so fucking annoying because the sane world truly sees and feels the suffering. A crazy, enthusiastic messenger from god is the last thing people need amongst the very real ruin.

The mania will crack and then everything will erupt. I'm frightened and falling apart and I see spiders that no one else sees, and taking my last Klonopin won't do a lot. At this point, probably nothing.

And if I survive that madness, if I don't slit my wrists or jump off a bridge or dive under a car, running from my psychosis, depression will take over. I will cry and lie still and do nothing but wait to die - sometimes using my last scraps of energy to pray to die.

My meds are a matter of life and death. They are for a lot of people. With the way America is turning, it feels like this nightmare that I play out in my mind sometimes might actually come true. That all of us crazies will lose access to the tools that keep us less crazy, so we'll wind up crying and yelling and laying down in front of our houses because we've got nowhere else to go. No pills in our medicine cabinets, no refills at the Rite Aid, no pills in our palms, not enough money to buy 1200 mg of Lithium for the night.

And the more I play out this scenario, imagining that this is our inescapable future, scheming how I'll ration my psychiatric drugs—my pill cutter becoming a priceless device—the more often I come to the part of the daydream where I have to confront myself with the truth that I WILL run out of meds. What will that be like? What will I be like?

And as I keep thinking about how someday soon there will be nothing left to take, I feel myself going legitimately crazy. Twirling through thoughts about this Trumpian hellscape makes me grow increasingly paranoid, it spikes my anxiety, the delusions are stacked too high behind my ears. I think about Trump's America and what it will look like and I think, *Maybe I should take fewer meds tonight. I've got to save them!*

I've got to plan for the end, as I know it. Keep my crazy ass afloat for as long as possible. Ration with a fevered passion. Less meds now means I'll last longer, I think. I become nervous and agitated and fidgety and hollow and depressed and lost and so beyond hope that even today's meds are becoming useless.

I'm bipolar and broken. Ahead of schedule.

It just feels like I'm practicing for what it's going to be like when I can't afford my meds anymore.

I wonder how long it will take me to snap.

Hmmm. I guess we'll see.

keep us

Holding his hand doesn't stop my head from spinning. It doesn't stop the swirling blur of a world with too many colors and sounds, vibrant and violent, saturated and sense-less, beautiful and broken, so many senses, so many overflowing emotions. But I'd melt away, slip and sink, drink and drown, climb and crash without him. His fingers intertwined with mine keep me anchored. Because this mind of mine is like a kite. I fly and flail, I fumble and flutter, I flicker and fall into the madness that is my wind. I push and pull away from the sanity of this planet, my bipolar begging to thrust me into space. I'm always at risk of drifting into the clouds so I can come crashing down after. He understands.

He circles his fist around my wrist and I sway in the sky that is my bipolar, but I don't get whisked away. I'm attached to his fingertips, and he whispers in my shivering ears that he will always hold me close, especially when I rattle and roar, I dance and demand, I wonder and weep, when I threaten to pull away, push back, and let go so I can succumb to the crazy - to surrender to the maddening atmosphere, to the symphony of symptoms, rioting and rebelling into the ozone until I'm all used up and rocketing back towards the earth. Defeated and dented. And he understands.

I am lucky. I am lucky that he loves me and that it keeps me human. He loves me even when I look more like sickness than his wife. His love keeps me from being carried away completely, reminding me that I am alive no matter how hard I might fight and fly, I might tug and twist, I might want to run away to the corners of my crazy sky, tricked by the disease in me that speaks to sabotage and suffering.

He loves me and he understands. And love without understanding can quickly be lost. Undermined by miscommunication and mistakes. Jeopardized by symptoms that don't make sense. He loves me and he understands that, to some degree, my brain will always bend and break in the breeze, that I will always have moments of thunder and thoughtful-ness, that I will always live with an illness that keeps me climbing into the sky and then rips me right out of the blue so I plummet to the pavement. It's a back and forth for me, a fluid exchange between sanity and capsizing, the ups and downs of mental illness. It's life for us. It's hard, but I know I won't leave because he won't let me. Love keeps us close. Within arms reach. I am safe even as I soar. Even when I fall from the sky, he's always there. And he knows I will always be by his side, because no matter how hard I may shake and shudder, ripple and rage, crescendo and collapse, love and understanding keep us connected.

manic benders
and government contracts

I graduated from the University of Virginia in 2007 with a BA in psychology, an inflated sense of self-esteem, and a small collection of semi-regrettable tattoos. While I loved the quaint college town of Charlottesville, with diploma in-hand, I headed north, seeking employment, slinking into the belly of the D.C. area. This was a significant point in my life. Not only was I transitioning from "student" to "adult-hopeful with a career," but I was also reflecting on my goals, values, and overall sense of identity. I was on a mission to find a job that reflected who I was and aligned with my priorities. And a position I could be proud of. I was determined to successfully tackle this social milestone.

Okay, before you read on, let me preface this: I am a devout liberal, a relentless pacifist, and a hopeless humanitarian at heart. But, as you know by now, I am also bipolar, which means that consistency has never really been my thing. When I was looking for work that summer, I had two guideposts that ushered me along: my brand new diploma and the same old mania I'd been living with since I was fifteen. I soon learned that my mania, with its unyielding stamina and bottomless pit of "brilliant" ideas, excelled at sending out a shit ton of cover letters and resumes at breakneck speed to a very wide, undiscriminating continuum of potential employers, which is how I landed and accepted an internship with the Department of Defense…

What can I say? I guess I'll try anything once. Final words of an army of dumb-dumbs.

Great. So, we've established that mania is a talented catalyst when it comes to making bizarre, impulsive decisions (re: think semi-regrettable tattoos), but I also want to talk about how mania does a terrific job when it comes to stealing your memories. The nature of mania is that it revs up your brain to the point that it's so completely consumed with constant pulsing, vibrating, and rattling that it forgets to record what's going on in the world outside your chemically imbalanced jittery mind. Mania's ferocious energy can lead to reckless behavior, it can sabotage your relationships, it can jeopardize your safety, it can convince you to sleep with a republican econ major your sophomore year (like I said, I'll try anything once, but that is a story for another time), and it can ruthlessly wipe your mind clean - just like how it blanched my brain for the four month period I was a paid intern doing something or other for a government office. In these situations, finding artifacts* from your manic rainbow-outs** can help you connect at least some of the dots. I've been solving riddles for years. It's a big part of surviving bipolar disorder.

Quick pause for the words of the day:

*Artifacts: Clues you find after a manic episode that offer at least a glimpse of what happened when you were under the influence of your rampant manic bender. Since I was a teenager, I've relied on excavating for artifacts in order to piece together various clues to map out lost time. These artifacts manifest in a vast array of forms, but I am always eternally grateful whenever I can unearth them because their presence helps me feel less estranged from reality. In some cases, the artifact is a mammoth credit card bill. Or a dented car door. A truly trashed apartment. Semi-regrettable tattoos. An impulsive adoption of a little black kitten (her name is Juniper Montrieve and she's seven years old now). A reputation on campus that you're a slut. However, in most scenarios, artifacts are the stories you collect from other people. For me, artifacts confirm that I did, in fact, exist in a period where, in my mind, there is nothing but the leftover ash of old fireworks. Artifacts remind you that, even though you're crazy, you're still a human on planet Earth.

**Rainbow-outs: If you drink to excess, there is a very likely chance you'll blackout, brownout, greyout - you get the idea - which means you'll inevitably come to with a smattering of mystery bruises, a cracked iPhone screen, and a list of misplaced personal items, a hangover, and a very blurred, highly suspect recollection of the night before. Similarly, your brain on mania can produce gaps in linear and temporal timelines, which can span a few days, weeks, months, and, for some people, even years. The longest I've gone without logging any memories is about four months. This memory loss is the result of your unmedicated, addled brain marinating in magnetic neuro-chemical manic glitchiness for far too long. This pathological state of being transforms everything you encounter into being too vibrant, too saturated, too kinetic, and too exaggerated. Your senses - your whole system - is inundated with overwhelming color and unbridled energy; the majesty of unchecked mania causes you to gloriously and dramatically *rainbow-out*. But while alcoholics are saddled with next day headaches, bipolars crash into a depression. To sum it all up, alcoholics blackout when they drink too much, bipolars rainbow-out when our brains are irreversibly steeped in mania. While both may seem fun at first, they are dangerous in the long run. Cautionary tale: Must I remind you, a lapse in sanity and suddenly I was working for the Department of Defense!

Anyway, where was I?

Thanks to my raging, kaleidoscope, caving-in mania, I don't remember much from my four months spent interning at the Department of Defense, and I figured I never would. It would be yet another time period sacrificed to mania, an outcome I have learned to accept. But the other day, my husband stumbled upon a treasure when he was digging around in our old hard drives. Eureka! An artifact from August of 2007! A "research paper" I wrote entitled "Clan of Xymox: Harbingers of World Change and Instillers of International Tranquility," which, upon reading, I suddenly remembered submitting - very proudly in fact - to my boss at the DOD. Your American tax dollars at work (sorry!). At the time, was I obsessed with the Clan of Xymox, a Dutch rock band formed in 1981? Highly unlikely. I am fairly certain I never listened to any of their songs that summer, and I know for a fact I haven't since. Did the Department of Defense ever do business with the Clan of Xymox? I'm going to give that a hard no. Looking back, sane-me isn't sure why authoring this paper and giving it to my boss was a good idea, but I know manic-me knew it was an absolutely brilliant idea. Probably the best idea I'd ever had. And as I scrolled through the paper, I un-expectedly retrieved two other surviving details from that summer, both about my boss: 1) He was a republican, and 2) he was an aspiring comedian, the latter of which probably made my Xymox stunt seem more quirky than crazy. Finally some clues, or at least mementos.

And this is why artifacts can be a source of revelation for people living with bipo-lar. While my diploma states that I graduated from UVA and my work history shows that I interned at the DOD, there was obviously more to my life than that. For every rainbow-out episode I've experienced, I've managed to piece together a loose narrative based on stories from friends, stubs from airplane tickets, the number of condom wrappers wedged under my mattress, often abysmal school or work related attendance records, and freshly inked tattoos. Even though in these scenarios I'm sick, it is still me. For better or for worse, illness is a part of me that I recognize - part of my identity that has shaped my values and goals, that has nurtured my creativity. Finding my manic-fueled unofficial capstone project for the Department of Defense, "Clan of Xymox: Harbingers of World Change and Instillers of International Tranquility," provided evidence that the human part of me was there that summer; that I was underneath the shadow of my rainbow.

So, without further ado, below are some excerpts from my masterpiece. Peek into my rainbow and have a chuckle. Aw, what the hell, go look up the Clan of Xymox and let them serenade you as you read. I can't vouch for how good or bad they are. I still haven't listened to them yet.

In 1989, the album "Twist of Shadows" was released and 300,000 copies were sold. The release of this tectonic plate shiftingly good album caused positive aftershocks that rippled through the world. Though no causal proof exists, it is commonly believed that the release of this album triggered the fall of the Berlin Wall, the birth of the Game Boy, motivated the San Francisco 49ers to win Super Bowl XXIII, and served as the catalyst behind the on-air fight between guests on Geraldo Rivera's talk show that resulted in the host's nose being broken. Although the only obvious similarity between these events and the release of "Twist of Shadows" is that they all occurred in 1989, it is clear that these "coincidental" events were the product of "Twist of Shadows'" taking the world by storm.

Xymox created timeless music that was appreciated not only through the mediums of song and dance but also video games. In 1996, Xymox provided the soundtrack for the game Total Mayhem, and in 1997, they blessed the game-makers of Revenant with permission to use their vocals and instrumentals. Despite never having been officially involved with video games before this, do take into consideration that the advent of the Game Boy occurred in the same year as the release of "Twist of Shadows" and, thus, most likely, the band spawned the evolution of video games and gaming technology as we know it. Inspiring the creation of the Game Boy and then later furthering the progress of gaming by providing musical soundtracks, Xymox was a dynamic force in our technological world.

Not only was Xymox responsible for the evolution of modern gaming technology as we know it, but Xymox was also influential in rekindling the friendship between two feuding nations. Since WWII, Germany and the United States had been enveloped in tension and a mutual misunderstanding. Despite the German language having many cognates and thus being remarkably similar to English, Germany and the United States of America failed to find common ground and repair their damaged relationship. This was until Xymox was changed to the Clan of Xymox once again and signed with the German and U.S. record label, Tess Records. This marks the birth of the repaired German–U.S. relationship, which is why now each nation complacently tolerates the other from across the sea and shares a musical language, the lyrics of the Clan of Xymox.

In conclusion, be they the Clan of Xymox or just plain old Xymox, the musical brilliance is still the same. Cited as the "main producers of modern-day peace anthems for our troubled world" by me, the Clan of Xymox reaches out to the emo-punk roustabout within us all while preaching world peace. Marked by a tumultuous history of Game Boys, Super Bowl victories, Berlin Wall falls, lady astronauts, broken Geraldo Rivera noses, and racial equality, musical mastery is the legacy of the Clan of Xymox. But theirs is a story not yet complete. The sun has not yet set on these messiahs of sound, for the future is bright, bright with XYMOX!

confrontation

My body is a beautiful confrontation.
My nipples clench into tight, rosy fists.
Brown freckles spatter my skin,
body armor from my forehead to pinky toes.
Curves that intoxicate with desire
and enrage by refusing to hide.
Crooked teeth that can cut through the quiet.
Blue eyes that forgive, forget, and fervently find the good.
Thick fingers crowned with red-tipped talons that type out dissertations.
A brain that is brimming with bipolar,
but is also smart as fuck.
Let me remind you,
my body is beautiful.
She is strong, sweet, and armed to the teeth.
Never forget that she belongs to me.
I fight for this skin.
I am unapologetically my own.
Don't even dare to doubt me.
I'm all that I need.

clawing out
of my prescribed O grave

My head *tips* and *topples* over, dropping heavy lids to cover glazing eyes that see only outlines marred by f u z z y patches of medicine bottles topped with cotton. The too heavy lumbering numbness of over-medication reminds me of being alive but thinking I am dead. To pry your eyes open and clear your cobwebbed mind takes more energy and effort than you have because this new mood stabilizer flirting with your old antipsychotics subdues you with its crushing weight of fogginess that promises you'll be reassuringly asymptomatic.

Asymptomology comes at a price because your life blurs and trudges forward but you lose track of which day, and what time, and why am I here when I feel nothing, due to the spider webs braided into your dulled nerves. The damage this medication does to my sense of self, my perceptual framework of what makes me, me, is devastating as everything becomes *muted* and *subdued* under layers of valproic acidity that corrodes the corners of my brain where *Rachel* was forced to hide.

I'm sure on the outside it looked like I slipped willingly to sleep and I was comforted by my silence. But the silence was never mine, it was never *peaceful*. The silence was a sentence.

For a while, my heart and eyes tried to scream to save me from this unasked for slurred lull in my life, this medicated, suffocated nightmare that took away my brightness. But I was sentenced. And it wasn't that I ever grew comfortable, but I grew to feel nothing at all, so I did myself a favor by letting all my thoughts fall into line, sinking slowly into what some would call a pattern of laziness, of *lethargic resignation*. But I called it **self**-preservation because I didn't know what else to say.

I became complacent to the medication and surrendered to the thought that this is what it took to render me harmless to myself. No longer a psychotic threat to my own wellbeing, but now an eighteen-year-old lump of sad, toppled teenager who forgot it was even possible to live a better life. That she deserved a better life where her illness didn't own her and her medication didn't make her nothing more than mere puddles on the floor because all she could do was sit and struggle to lift her foggy lids while she forgot herself. Imprisoned by a Depakote-fueled case of Stockholm Syndrome, captive of a drug that whispered to her…

That this was how life had to be with her disorder because *Rachel* was just too sick to own her thoughts.

I still wake up startled sometimes because I'm afraid I don't have permission to think again; that my thoughts will be old and muddied, dragging themselves through the dirt of my mind, and all I can do is watch them and feel *sheer terror* as I realize that my brain must be gone. When I am jolted from this nightmare and I enter the liminal space where I exist between sleeping and being awake, in this disoriented holding cell, I panic at the thought of losing my shiny ideas that once paraded around my brain as well constructed cognitions wrapped in ribbons. I refuse to be over-medicated again. I refuse to fall into the drooling daily mechanics of psychomotor retardation. Never again will I succumb to the pharmaceutical-submissive patient relationship modeled after capture bonding.

I forgot myself for over a year before. I was stolen from my own head.

Too many medications in an insecure high school body.

Those days remain *blurry bubbles* of a terrifying cognitive paralysis. I still am somewhat haunted by these memories, fear that I will be silenced and stripped of my thoughts again, but am thankful that for now I can wake up, and I can think, and I remember who I am and why I love to be her. So I will speak up and fight to protect my brain, both from suffocating under a deluge of excessive pills or straying too far into the crazy brushfire of my illness.

I want to keep myself where I can see her.

in the end

I don't live with consequences,

not in my bipolar world.

Whether I'm manic or depressed,

I either don't have the need for them or they don't even exist.

I've never worried about what happens next, or if next even happens.

When I'm manic, everything is so vibrant and loud and brilliant and lovely that nothing can go wrong. I'm an electric genius who is always right and always beautiful and every decision I make, every shortcut I take, is driven by my divine design. No step is ever a stumble, no question ever goes unanswered. I'm confident and cocky and delightfully crazy—so crazy that it's a compliment because I'm better and beyond everyday people and everyday ideas. I know what's best for everyone and everything. The universe is my instrument and I know what songs to play and when to play them - how often, how frantic, how fevered, which voices to drown out and how loud to sing my solo.

Nothing I do is a mistake, everything is my intentional spectacle.

There are no consequences because I am always, always, alive and on fire,

dazzling and crackling and sparkling and shining,

and I am *always* convinced I will *always* be this way.

Mania has no need for a future when right now is so violently heavenly.

I'm not at the mercy of human aftermath.

Consequences need not apply.

Too perfect to be punished.

When I'm depressed, there are no consequences because I don't care what happens next.

Consequences are inconsequential.

I don't care if I live or die, I don't care if I drown or dehydrate, if I burn to death or am buried alive, I don't care if I'm trampled or abandoned, if I'm full of sorrow or empty and aching.

I just don't care about tomorrow,

or the next day or the day after that, because I will always feel this wretched and worthless, this disgusting and devalued, and there is no world in which I will ever be okay. I don't care about consequences because I am a mistake who will always slip and trip and fall into miserable nothingness. I'm stuck in a mire of hopelessness and self-loathing and even the thought of getting a tomorrow is a sign of grace I don't deserve.

And I am *always* convinced I will *always* be this way

With depression, consequences don't exist because I can't escape the pain of right now.

Too destroyed to deserve a second chance.

Consequences mean nothing and everything.

Manic or depressed, I'm stuck in my madness,

perpetually captured in one cycle or another.

There are no consequences.

There are no changes.

There is no what happens next.

There is only bipolar.

And me falling apart at the poles.

my manic opus

Mania requires music that speaks only to you.

Music that vibrates along your jawline, shooting lyrical echoes to the back of your throat as they cut lattice lines down your spine.

Kind of like an animated xylophone in a cartoon from the eighties, oversized Glockenspiel mallets with gumdrop tips clunking out a simple, comedic tune. Except with mania, the pace is reckless, the mallets hammer out chaotic sounds that wreak havoc in your too-tight chest.

Not enough room to direct the ricochet.

My manic playlist rattles my teeth; my tongue clashes into my cheeks and nudges blood from my gums. The hollow of my throat is clogged with too much intoxicating noise.

The songs I savor on my iTunes playlist are played loudly and repeatedly.

Grimes first, Miike Snow up next, "What is Love" by Haddaway played six or seven times in a row, Kid Cudi "Pursuit of Happiness (Extended Steve Aoki Remix) feat MGMT and Ratatat"

LOUDLY,

anything written by OK Go is sent spinning around my skull, but it is never just the song - I always watch the music videos until my eyes flake desperate and dry - then Toadies' "Possum Kingdom," which I sing at the top of my lungs, followed by "Call" by Francesco Yates, which makes me sway and slide and pull my hair out, and Sia is probably crazy like me—just look at her—I celebrate this revelation within myself as her music leaks through my keyboard,

and lastly, "Malibu" by Hole, which isn't exactly easy on the ears, but the lines stick in my ribs, snug like a life preserver...

"I can't be near you, the light just radiates"—I AM THE LIGHT.

How did Courtney *Love* know? We haven't met yet. I am so loud that my lungs rip right open, but I don't need to breathe or sing or even laugh because I feel everything at once in a way so elegant only Daft Punk's electronic mash-ups understand.

The hairs on the back of my neck bristle and my eyes are dry and brittle because I've pried them open for three days straight.

Sleep is for the silent. I have too much noise in my ears.

Claire Elise Boucher aka Grimes sedates me with her music. I feel wild inside and my mind races with colorful ideas, but I am stuck in my seat.

Lodged into this wooden chair, like my spine is a javelin—only seconds ago, thrown in an arch through the clouds, piercing my ceiling, sliding cleanly into my skull, severing my sanity as it pins me to the ground.

I think about Phineas Gauge, cut quickly by a railroad iron and left for crazy—he died at thirty-six and I'm thirty-one. I have to be careful.

But what an attractive man, especially with one eye. Look him up. You're welcome. But all I can do is cast my eyes toward the white painted ceiling overhead and let hot tears slither down my cheeks.

Grimes was going to be a neuroscientist until she was expelled from McGill University for making too much music. A busy little twinkling alien who really gets me.

And Kid Cudi has depression. I saw it in a Buzzfeed article so it must be true.

Someone tweeted this sentiment that I'm struggling to paraphrase—my mind is too busy whistling—"If this is the music he writes when he's sick, I can't wait to hear his work when he's healthy." But will *I* relate to a Kid Cudi that's patched up?

I can't even keep my own Band-Aids in place. My brain gets too wet and warm and they wriggle away. I'm allergic to the adhesive anyway; plastic sutures make my skin blister.

And Courtney Love didn't commit suicide, her husband did, and when I'm MANIC as fuck, I can't remember his name because he doesn't matter as much to me—I think about Courtney *LOVE* and how her daughter Frances Bean *HATES* her.

Pushing people away is a well-established characteristic of my disease.

BUT I FEEL SO GOOD when I pulsate and the music dissects and pricks apart the fleshy warm wiggling pile of pink pus in my head that I call a brain.

Quick hands wheedle pushpins into the part of the cerebral cortex that urges me to make bad decisions. Plotting out prime real estate in the gelatinous tissue, leaving place markers at the craziest parts so I can go back and poke them later, sell segments off to somebody. Combing through the goo, leaving thumb prints on the softest spaces in my skull, prying open the grey matter to see who else is creeping inside.

I feel feral and wonderful and I want to take a scissor to my hands because, at this point in my manic episode, my blood must sparkle. My body is tense and I punch the floor, where I am slumped, because I fell from my chair—my skeleton forgetting how to keep me upright.

To my dismay, I haven't yet bloodied a single knuckle.

I'm not on drugs, I'm on bipolar, and she is cruel, beautiful, and engineered to make me soar and crash for eternity.

Like a playlist set on an everlasting loop.

Twenty One Pilots calls their music "schizoid pop," and maybe that name is offensive, but the lyrics sure are catchy as hell as I scream them into my fists. They do have a point.

And as Kehlani looks lovingly into the microphone and blasts her ballad "CRZY" right in its face, all I can say is that this anthem made her more of an "assassin," confessing to all of us that "I go I go I go I go…" and everything she does, she does with passion, killing them with compassion, and we both tried to kill ourselves.

What are the odds that she sees me through the speakers?

But somehow she knows I'm going going going going CRZY, too. We are one in the same, but her stomach is tighter and her tattoos send more of message. But it's hard to decipher her designs over Google image. Maybe we will meet in real life and I will see the secrets inked in her neck tattoo.

I sing "Possum Kingdom"—"be my lover, be my lover"—and—"What is Love"—because what the fuck is (Courtney) LOVE if it isn't this illness that worships me and then tries to kill me?

But I love my madness anyway. Isn't love about forgiveness?
I forgive you bipolar. I love you mania!

I feel like throwing up, but I haven't eaten food in days—my cheeks bleed where I've bitten them into swollen, crusted cubbyholes. I taste like red salt and nobody loves me but my mania. Every lyric makes sense and I am let down by real people who say real things off beat.

I just know that each artist left me a line scrawled in invisible ink that is dedicated just to me and it whispers my innermost thoughts and it flickers in the music videos that I drool over.

My mania is delectable, and these songs incite the fire in my mind, taunting my tantrum, and nothing will extinguish me because I can't let it go.

Too stubborn to share my omnipotence. My jaw is locked territorially tight around my transcendent melodies.

Just one more listen to the playlist because I might have missed something crucial, critical, a key piece of my bloody, mentally ill puzzle.

I push scissors into my skin to keep me real and on the floor, and Sia shatters my skull with a waterfall of diamonds. I borrow perfect words from Francesco Yates, "I don't ever want to be lonely with no one else," and I try to sing them to my sweet mania, but she's too busy choking the life out of me.

And before I pass out from electric, livid bliss, before the sequined reaper looming over me kicks me in the chest with her iridescent spiked pearl boot, my favorite poet, ee cummings, reminds me of the verse he wrote especially for me, for situations like these,

"Shake the mountains when *YOU* dance," and I tremble

with the ferocity of an infinite sickness, and I laugh at my momentum, which hurls my body into nothingness, and maybe I'll find my way back if I follow the trail of droplets of tears and blood and music that is growing fainter by the second, threatening to leave me behind in this disease.

But often times, there is nothing I can do but pray someone fiddles with my volume.

Because my hands are pinned by mania's pearlescent shit-kickers as she spits psychosis down my swollen throat - a pink puffed aching tunnel that sang much too loudly, too desperately, too foolishly in an attempt to woo her.

A failed attempt to enchant her, capture her, make her mine.

And then psychosis comes to stay, and she whittles paper doll chains out of my brain and hangs them all around my psychiatrist's office. Playful bloody madness dressed as delicate shapes slammed on his white walls. The stains set in and I just know insurance won't cover it.

the *ephemeral opulence* of this illness

Bipolar poems keep me up at night. Brilliant ideas keep my brain bubbling. Neurotransmitter parties every evening keep me more creatively awake than obediently asleep. Who needs this restful quiet when the serotonin speaks to me so sweetly?

My ideas - bright, barbed nettles with radiant points - rattling around in my brain, quickly ricocheting off my smooth skull, like shining marbles. Flickering phantoms too fascinating to exist for long.

I wake up to witness purple petals with tiny lit centers floating from between my eyelids, forming suspended circles of elegantly natural lavender light that spirals outward and upward into grey clouds of nothing.

Breathing in music and love,
like candlelit sea urchins bathing in my overflowing lungs.

The neighborhood bricks disintegrate into diamond dust. Cutting corners into crystals. My manic mind is a bright, pulsing light bulb. It is energy. It is kinetic. Its glittery brilliance transmits honest light throughout my body. See brightness.

And then the psychosis kicks in.

THREE

psychosis

the *night* my cat told me to *kill myself*

my husband had gone back to California for business.

The last time he was away, things unraveled quickly. Looking back, I've been trying to pinpoint the specific moment in time when my brain decided that life wasn't worth the hassle. I'm still not exactly sure when I broke.

It was November in Pittsburgh, which means it was cold and dark. If there had been any snow on the ground, it was grey and used at that point, and no one was excited about it. I had been alone for about a week, and my husband was due back soon. It seems odd when I look back now because I was so close to the finish line. I was so close to seeing him again and having everything make sense. But instead, I fell apart.

I guess there wasn't a singular "moment" at all. There were a series of weird moments. I started getting weird, which progressed into becoming even weirder. And then I was definitely at my weirdest.

My weirdest thoughts are the most dangerous. They are obscure and alarming, and they don't make sense to me, but they are the only semblance of sense that I have left. I'm left with nothing but my disturbing, weird ideas and my stifling anxiety I can't explain. Often, there is no one there to listen.

When I reach this point, rife with unease and short circuits, I operate like a defective robot. I am distant and numb, my movements are jerky, and I don't think on my own.

But nobody has programmed me to do anything at all so I just continue getting weirder.

I guess a more accurate word than "weird" would actually be "psychotic," but that sounds so apocalyptically condemning and pathological. I feel like when people hear that someone is "psychotic," they think that this individual is a knife-wielding maniac with no conscious or soul or capacity for remorse. This person wants to hurt others for odd, scary reasons. This person is just violent and crazy. This person cannot be saved.

I always wonder what this person looks like.

It is hard to know what other people think, but that November, the psychotic person looked like me. And while I know it wasn't truly "me," because my therapist always reassures me that it is just my illness taking over, it is still my mind and my body and my pain. Which makes it that much harder to run away.

I was not a knife-wielding maniac. I had a conscience and a soul. I was remorseful. I didn't want to hurt others for odd, scary reasons. But I was crazy. And I felt violent towards myself because I could not be saved.

When you are at that place, when sanity has flaked away, and you are left bare and splintered, you only have the crazy thought that you cannot be saved. And you cling to it. Because honestly, it doesn't sound all that crazy.

You are so lost and gone, and you look in the mirror and you see blue bewildered eyes, but they aren't yours, even though they are anchored deep in your pale face. And you stare in the mirror for hours and you try to find out who you are, but your freckles don't listen and they shift when you blink, so you have to start counting them all over again.

If you just knew how many freckles… Maybe it would be you…

And your lips do whatever they want, and your hair doesn't listen because you aren't really there anymore. You have no control.

And you can't be saved.

That is the one thing - the only thing - that you know.

And while you may have a few fleeting moments when you wonder if that is true, that you are really doomed, suddenly your freckles move again and you are beyond lost, buried in a labyrinth of neurochemical glitches. The hope goes out.

That November, I had a microphone in my tooth and everyone was listening to me. And they knew I could not control my freckles and they wanted to take my eyes because they were never mine—they were just stuck in my head. And I didn't want them to listen to me, and while I wasn't sure who "they" were, I knew that we all agreed on something. Just one thing.

I could not be saved.

So, even though Princess Diana told me I shouldn't, I put all my medication in a cup. Every pill in the cabinet. When I went to open the medicine cabinet, I first had to look at its front surface… the mirror. And the mirror looked back at me, and my lips, which did whatever they wanted, smiled and told me it was okay to let go. And my hair was wild and frightening and it just wouldn't listen, and Princess Diana had perfect hair so who was she to tell me what to do when she clearly had no idea what I was going through?

And my freckles kept disappearing. Little lights flickering out before my stolen eyes.

I put all my pills in a cup—pills that were supposed to keep me from feeling crazy, pills that were supposed to help me think and help me sleep and make me feel like I might be saved one day if I just worked hard at it and did what my doctor said. But it was too late, because they didn't work, and I didn't work… I broke.

I am not sure who exactly, but someone who I had spoken to - maybe it was my therapist, or my husband, or Princess Diana - had called a friend to come check on me.

And my friend thought I could be saved.

She didn't say it, but I saw it in her nervous smile, and she looked me in the eye and she didn't say a word about my chaotic freckles. Then my parents came the next morning. Then my husband came home. And we put the pieces back together.

But then my husband went back to California for business.

I was alone again. It was May. I could do it this time.

There was no pitiful snow, only uncut, wild grass. I really, earnestly believed that I could do it. I had a plan now and saw my therapist twice that week, and I cuddled my dogs and I tamed my hair.

It was going to be fine.

But I was lonely. And food tasted weird. I figured I would just eat light because my stomach always acts up when I'm nervous. So I ate crackers and tried some soup. I drank bubble tea because it was sweet and simple. And that was all I needed in my life - for things to be sweet and simple.

It was Wednesday night and my husband was due back late on Friday. And I cried myself to sleep because the bed was deep and empty. Thursday was full of rain and I couldn't swallow the lump stuck in my throat. It stuck there and felt uncomfortable and even the bubble tea wouldn't dissolve it. The dogs were loud and had unbridled energy, and I was just hopeless and tired.

It is hard to remember everything. I know that Thursday was terrible and I canceled plans with friends because I didn't understand why they would want to see me. I had left the dogs at doggy daycare because it hurt to see their exuberance when all I could do was cry and collapse.

Friday, I sat with my cats. I sat with my cats and they listened and purred. And I wept and I ached and I didn't understand why I had to be alone. But my husband was coming home that night and I knew I could do it this time. His plane was due at 10 p.m., and I wanted him to call. I knew if I heard his voice, I would feel better and the blackness would start to pull back from my brain. But he didn't call. I worried and wondered and the minutes ticked by. Now it was 10:30 p.m.

And I knew he was dead.

I was frantic and confused. I felt a stab in my chest and the lump in my throat grew five sizes bigger so I could barely breathe. *What would I do without him?*

But my freckles didn't jump so maybe this time I would be okay and maybe I could be saved after all…

I sat with my cat and she looked at me with gentle brown eyes. I asked her why she wouldn't answer my prayers and where was Princess Diana this time? And while I knew the microphone was no longer in my tooth, it didn't matter because they were not my eyes and I knew it. My cat was right.

So, I put on my sandals and went outside. My husband called, his plane had been delayed, but I knew it wasn't really him. He told me he would be home soon and that he loved me. But cats are smart and they have nine lives so they have a lot of experience with living. My cat was right, because why should I live in a world where my husband could die at any moment? It is such a shame we just have one life so we can't even practice living.

That night, I realized that within the span of one tiny life you could easily lose the person who means the most to you. You could watch them slip into the gnawing nothingness that claims all of us, save for Earth's collection of cats. Your world comes crashing down into heaps of smoldering rubble, thick tar pits of broken black and glass. *Was life even worth it?* Maybe my husband was on the phone right now, but he was going to die at some point.

It felt like a dream.

It wasn't a nightmare because I felt calm as I walked to the bridge.

It all made sense.

I didn't have to hurt, and this is how I could be saved. I was psychotic, but I was worth saving, and I could save myself if I just jumped and flew and let the world go. And I knew I was close to the finish line because he was driving towards me in his blue Subaru and he was saying nice things and how he would come and get me; how we would figure things out, because we were always in a state of figuring things out.

But I was tired of finish lines and I couldn't run anymore. I wanted to break apart.

I was a block away, but I didn't make it to the bridge.

Luckily, he caught me just in time and he told me I was never broken. He whispered to me that life is easier when we have each other to love. Even with a brain prone to glitches.

I didn't believe him, but I did start to feel safe again.

as i slump to the side

Bipolar hijacks my mind sometimes. I have to think about it, manage it every day, but with the right pills and the right bed time, I can usually keep my head together. But sometimes I can't. And when everything frays and my mind threatens to fall to pieces, and especially the times it fucking erupts, I'm thankful for the love in my life that hugs me together and props me upright. The world spins on as I slump to the side, but there are always people holding my hand and I'm never forgotten, even when I'm lost for a while.

Why am I so crazy?
I ask everyone and no one knows,
or maybe they just don't want to tell me.
"I can take it!" I yell from the ceiling.

Why am I so crazy?
My psychiatrist clicks out a prescription for some kind of med
to be sent to the pharmacy at the end of the street,
where the pharmacist knows me by name
and exactly where the plastic bag with my new bottle swings from the rack,
like a translucent bat that swallowed my self-care and doesn't mind the fluorescent lights.
"What is wrong with me?"
I cry and coo and try to exclaim without sounding so crazy
that the prescription becomes a trip to the hospital
My psychiatrist blinks and my pharmacist clinks pills into a plastic cylinder.
They say to me, "Have a nice day."

Why am I so crazy?
I ask my mom and my dad and we look at our gnarled family tree,
where the roots are solid but the branches are thin.
Mental illness is our pollen, sampled from ancestors across the canopy,
then sprinkled generously on flower after flower of fucking crazy.

Kallems and Shelmandines
and Oppenheims
and Kerrs

And all those other decaying names that I can't recall or maybe I never knew.
I wish I could conjure up my dead grandparents to ask them why they were crazy
and why they slipped pollinated poison into my skull,
where it blooms in my brain and itches my eyeballs,
an allergy to my family.

Why am I so crazy?
One sister texts me back with emojis and empathy and concern
and the distance from Arlington to Pittsburgh.
One sister doesn't answer my calls,
but she tries so hard to treat me kindly, even though I make her crazy,
but she doesn't know why I am a lunatic, she just knows that I take up a lot of time.
They both do.

Why am I so crazy?
My husband smiles soft and traces my hands, holds my heart, keeps me from running out
the front door, looking for an explanation in the middle of the street.
"Why am I like this?"
I say to his mouth and watch his words struggle to fall out.
He has no answers, just blind reassurance in the shape of, "You're going to be okay."
Like I would believe it.

Why am I so crazy?
The dogs don't know.
The cats don't know.
The rabbit that lives under our porch doesn't give a shit.
And the back alley has rats who could care less.
Our neighbors have a garden next to our fence and the flowers freak me out
with their wide petals and strong smells,
and the fact that they trespass in our yard, teasing our dogs, and choking my air.
They make me feel like a monster because all I want to do is rip them out of the ground
since their only purpose is to huddle together and say, "I love you," or, "I'm sorry,"
and I don't fucking care.
I just want to know why I'm batshit.

Why am I so crazy?
I can't find answers engraved on my fingertips.
I can't find riddles on the soles of my feet.
The ditch of my elbows are empty, and the backs of my knees are cowards.

I am covered in tattoos, but they aren't hieroglyphics.
They're just a collection of black and grey images.
They're blueprints of my body, but all they map is pain and pleasure and the part of me
that remembers how hurting can feel so good when you hate yourself.
I walk down the street and people say, "Nice ink," and I wince
because the second my skin falls, off no one will want to talk to me anymore.

Why am I so crazy?
Everyone else knows what to do and who they are.
Maybe they don't know why they are this way or act this way,
but they don't care because they fit in,
and I fucking fall out because I'm crazy and I can't fix it,
because I don't know why this is inside me,
or how to remove it.
Everything festers when you're fucking insane.

Why am I so crazy?
My psychiatrist
My pharmacist
My parents
My sisters
My husband
The dogs, the cats, the rats, and that dumpy brown rabbit
The beheaded flowers
The people on the sidewalk
The woman at the bank
The cashier at Target
The guy chipping ham in the deli section
all look at me with suspicious white eyes and I don't blame them
because the frequency of my thoughts is too chaotic
and crowded
and cyclical
and oh yeah

CRAZY
But I don't know why.

love is never having to say you're sorry for psychosis

He knew me with anorexia.

He had a sense of my bipolar.

He felt the anxiety.

He saw the scars and the tears.

But neither of us knew the psychosis.

But it seemed to know me.

My teeth rattled with microphones carved into my molars, my hair fell out because it wasn't mine, my freckles shook and squirmed across my pale skin, my tongue didn't feel at home in my mouth, my eyes were red-rimmed and raw and too big for my face, my ears caught wind of whistling and murmuring that no one else seemed to hear, and my fingernails fell off, one by one, fluttering like rose petals to the ground. I cried and rocked and begged for angels or death or both, and I was so confused, I couldn't look in the mirror. Because I knew the girl staring back at me was a watery hallucination. A fractured dream with a pale pained face that couldn't be saved by pills, or therapy, or love. Or anyone.

This was me now.

I sat on the floor in the kitchen, curled up by the corner of the couch, laid across the cool tiles of the bathroom, and pawed the scratches on my bedroom floor. No matter where I went, where I sought shelter, I never felt safe from the wings thrashing inside my brain. I couldn't escape the itch of my skin, couldn't sate the desire to fillet my own wrists. I drowned in the metallic taste souring my mouth. I was mired in the quicksand of the crazy, sick lump settling in my stomach. I heard my own death muttered between my red, bitten lips. I closed my eyes and saw unstable constellations of madness flickering across my lids. To be that damaged. To feel that empty and that overwhelmed. To be that fucking crazy.

This was so new.

I cry so violently when I'm sick. Even when he holds my hand and presses his lips against my temple. I cry because I am frightened, and even though he sits beside me, I feel so alone. He feeds me packaged food because I'm being poisoned, he counts my pills because I don't trust them, he sits with me in the kitchen, by the couch, leans against the the bathroom door, and leads me to our bed. He tells me he will watch me while I sleep to prevent the world from caving in. He tells me he loves me. The soundtrack of my sickness. His love and the rambled ranting of a brain on the brink of irreparable brokenness. He raises his voice to drown out the din of my disorder, to silence the lies of my spinning mind, to take back my brain with a chorus of *I love you's.*

And finally, when the illness breaks, like a psychotic fever that sheds disease and brings me back to my brain, I look into his quiet eyes, his eyebrows no longer curved in concern, before I tell him I love him. I tell him that I'm sorry.

"Why are you sorry, hun?"

"Because I fall apart and you have to take care of me. I am crazy beyond repair. How can you live your life when my disorder takes over? I'm sorry."

"This isn't your fault. It's part of our lives."

"But this psychosis. I feel unrecognizable. I feel like a burden. I'm sorry."

"You are not your disorder."

"I'm still sorry."

"Don't say you're sorry, just say that you love me because I love you more than anything. We're a good team, whatever we have to go through. I know sometimes you don't believe me, but that's when you need to listen to me the most."

"I love you."

"I love you, too."

I don't have to apologize.

I don't have to doubt my worth.

I'm not my psychosis.

I live with mental illness, but that doesn't mean I have to live with shame.

I live with love.

And love is enough to remind me who I really am.

And when I'm cursed and cluttered with craziness, he still sees me.

That's how we love.

anything else

Remember

It's so hard to sleep through the night,
despite new meds and old coping techniques,
slow breathing and fast acting benzos.
I still wake up with hands around my throat,
with ice seizing my veins and fire boring holes in my chest,
frozen and in flames, barricaded in the blankets,
everything feels so fucked up

Remember

I'm in my bed right now, but it feels like it's back then
and I'm back there, and everything's so goddamn backwards,
and I'm trying desperately to stay awake.
I can't close my eyes,
I can't roll over on my other side,
I can't graze my cheek across my pillow,
I can't nuzzle against the beating heart of my sleeping husband

Remember

I'd rather stay up all night with my brain aching from exhaustion.

I'd rather risk the sanity and light myself on fire.

I'd rather feel my skin sizzle with sweat and then burn with the chills

Remember

I just can't go back to bed and be expected to lie under the sheets,

hearing my heart scream, shrill and piercing and paralyzing,

I just can't go back to bed and be expected to sigh myself goodnight

when I'm locked in my mind and mired in memories.

I know I'm not back there, it's not back then, but it feels so real, so right now,

I can feel those hands on my throat

Remember

I can feel the burn and scorch, the heaviness and the horror.

I'm scratching at nothing but my own skin, and I'm bruised and frightened just like back then.

And just like back then, I can't move my limbs or make noise,

and I'm stuck in his house like I'm stuck in my bed,

and it's old tattered me in a new battered body, living a memory that refuses to die,

that comes on too fast and tortures so slowly

Remember

It's been a few weeks now and all I do is cry and lie awake at night.

I'm afraid to shut my fluttering eyelids,

so I stay watchful in my bed, clutching knees to my chest, and I hum into my ears.

The bedspread gnarled in my white clammy fingers that creak

when I dig too deep into pink sheets.

My body is raw and my sanity is flaking away, but

Remember

I'd rather go crazy than stay awake,

hide behind bipolar so I can stop remembering,

lose myself in old shades of psychosis instead of new twinges of terror.

I lull myself into comforting craziness.

I'm determined to die with my eyes open.

Anything, so I don't have to

Remember

to be a person

The inside of my cat's mouth looks like a bridge to Terabithia.
Tip-toeing on all fours, she pierces slick concrete with her molting talons.
She is sharp on every appendage except her tail that whips and quivers and silently rattles

– much like a snake –

– much like an anxious sigh –

– much like her own bristled whiskers -

Her eyes are wider than they should be, full of green flecks and leaves.
A purr like the early drumming of a storm.
When she sheds, I pick fur from my teeth.

I can see the flat line of my creased mouth mirrored in my dog's honey-brown eyes.
When she blinks, I start to wonder if the next mouth I'll see, bouncing back at me from the reflection anchored in her concerned, wet eyes, will be curved into a smile,
or maybe I'll see a frown as she sighs through a cold nose and we both curl against the carpet.
She winks with such softness, and I can hear my own heart thudding seemingly for nothing.
I wonder if I'm smiling.
Her eyelids glide open, and I see my colorless face cradled in my arms, with a mouth of someone who can't make up her mind,
emotionless and tired on the living room floor,
my chest rising and falling under the steady gaze of my dog
who understands the world better than me.

It is hard to be a person.

Bodies are hard, and I know that recovery isn't linear, but it is so agonizing when my anorexia aggressively haunts me.

I will never be enough.

Rachel,

please

be kind,

be patient,

and

believe

you are worthwhile

as you are.

the predictability of this
sickness

No breaks. No pause. Just cycling. Either actively in it or waiting for the next symptom. Always waiting and watching for the symptom to surface and ruin my understanding of how I can possibly live my life. Different medications, quickly shifting dosages, all in an attempt to catch the forceful moods, delusions, and feelings that start in my mind and spray like firecrackers into my heart or slowly slosh into my stomach, filling every emotional chasm with competing light and quicksand.

At times, I rupture so brightly that I see God and myself standing in the spotlight because I am transcendent, magnificent, and beautiful in every way. And then I slip and sink and feel myself drowning, choking on pain and dust, because I am a broken person who is only a leftover of her former brilliant self who now collects cobwebs in her lungs.

When I'm depressed like this, I just can't see. Sometimes tears leave track marks on my glasses, but sometimes my eyes are just dull. They are no longer full of light - not even a glimmer. Not even a dim glimmer that I can hope to resurrect because there is nothing but a hollow pit of loss and disease behind my eyelids.

I always run this race, I know this race so well. My mind throwing itself forward, waving its arms, hurtling faster and faster so it can outrun medicine and reason.

My mind reaches greedily and tragically for that psychotic finish line because if I just let it all go and the craziness seeps in and floods my body from toes to eyes and spills out on my glasses then you can see the track marks and I can escape into the madness that terrifies me and separates me from my skin.

My psychosis–steeped brain launches me into visions of Jesus eating my wrists, of police officers poisoning my orange juice with toxic flecks of unassuming pulp, of falling through the floorboards of my house to find a pit full of fangs and crossbows erected in my basement, of feeling my freckles burn holes in my skin until my eyes fall out, bypassing tear-covered glasses so that I can gently cradle each whimpering retina in the palms of my wrinkling hands as I dissolve them silently in my own hysteria.

Hurry up and wait for this inevitable insanity that I can't help but chase.

In between 600 and 800 mg of Seroquel is where I'll find sleep, says the man scrawling promises on the prescription pad.

So, I decide to stay cozied up next to a castle of capsules, just waiting for the increased dose to do the most good and knock me the fuck out; to follow the yellow pill road and find sleep waiting for me with open arms and a wide, dizzying smile.

I've spent too many nights in a row going back and forth in between shallow sleep and bad dreams.

The side effects of dehydration and confusion add to the exhaustion, and throughout the night, I gasp for water and cough up dust from too many tablets.

I know better, and I know by now, that the darkness will soon sludge into my skull, or the mania will grab me by the ears, rattling my mind until syrupy sparkles seep from my eyes, unless I fix the mess that is me.

I don't want to be sick, I'm trying to do the right things, but the 800 mg does nothing but lie and tease and brag and berate me all night long, calling me a gullible cunt, as it keeps sleep out of my reach.

What do I do when I've done everything they've told me to do? Deep breathing, slow yoga, thick pills, happy lamps, and yet I lie here, in a dungeon made out of a duvet, too stuck to seek out the sleep that needs me.

My sleep, sweet and soft, a damsel in distress, just waiting for me to free her from a prison of manic depression, subdued by a fever brought on by bipolar. It'll all be over if I can find her and bring her home;

slip her back into my skull where she will nestle and nuzzle into my brain, settling in between blankets and throw pillows and manageable doses of medication.

And she will close my eyes and steady my heartbeat and declutter my mind.

Her truth is much needed peace that sweeps across my forehead, fluttering my bangs and cooling my skin, leaving me easy and sighing.

The 800 mg will fall under her spell, and working together, things will start to go smoothly, unwrinkled, and well, and I'll take over bipolar and get back my life.

Sleeping seven hours a night.

I believe it will happen - as long as I hold on to the hope that one day there will be sleep and silence designed with my brain in mind.

Sleep and sanity are waiting for me.

vengeful lids

Me in psychosis.

The eyes inside me take photographs of my coiled, entangled layers of ribs and hearts and kidneys and lungs that push out bright flashbulbs of energy as the eyes outside me see the freckled teeth and wavy hair with eyebrows plucked into confusing knots that toss and turn over crooked lenses. Conveying no emotion, these eyes blink and blur - the inside eyes and the outside eyes - so I am rendered nothing but a sagging heap of moist circles that push their skin petal lids together despite being slurred by their heavy dripping lashes that dot each tragic lid. Vengeful lids promising one tear of coiled red blood that guarantees to reveal a silent picture of me in the dark room.

Me as a diagnosis.

My eyes are like opalescent eggs, and I sigh and slash them into crescent moons.

When I'm bipolar-tired, my skin cells scream and my teeth itch. The tips of my fingers ignite. The seeping tender pulp where my teeth are anchored in the halo of my mouth just begs to be picked apart by long, flaming fingernails.

I'm blurry at every corner, and my mind buzzes with radiation and it's like I'm sentencing myself to the electric chair and I don't even care. The zapping and spitting in my skull forces me awake, even though I'm exhausted and jam-packed with medication. I'm too tired to sleep. I'm wired against my will.

I lie in bed, and in an insomniac's stupor, I grab the soft fat on my stomach and I'm all about body checking myself throughout the night. I drift asleep, but suddenly wake up to pinch my excess pounds on my too big frame and it's like a nightmare. In the middle of bipolar nights, my anorexia narrates my dreams. The self-torture of squeezing my extra meat. The fear of fatness boring red-hot pokers into my eyes so I can't sleep in between the fire. If I fall asleep, I'll wake up and be fat.

I ferociously scratch my skin to see how it feels and the sound of my nails furrowing track marks in my forearm is like an odd, throbbing lullaby. I'm plowing crop circles in my skin and the wet hum of divining lazy blood rivers helps me keep time to the heaving of my madness. I whisper softly to myself in between the scratches—not sure of what I'm saying—but I can't slip into a sounder sleep. So I rip and pinch until my brain is evicted from this cluttered body. I grab my worn, weeping suitcases and go. I don't get my deposit back because there's too much damage. The before and after scratches are too severe.

The next-day medication hangover is brutal. I took pill after pill, stocked like a Pez dispenser, but it didn't deliver the sleep I signed up for, so I'm infuriatingly fuzzy from the sedative powers of my white tablets - usually my white knights, the Seroquel I thought I could trust. My eyelids are dredged open and I peek out of my jittery slits. My slimy eyes are vibrating like I plugged my lashes into a wall socket. I needed sleep and I didn't get it and the meds in me that failed to do their job still linger in the front of my brain, weighing it down with wet lies, and I'm so frustrated and sick. My bipolar giggles in the empty chamber of my mouth and my anorexic ideas strangle me so no food can get in.

I am awake.

Nobody look at me.

these *pills,* this *sleep*

Protect your sleep.

The psychiatrist on the other side of my eyes tells me that keeping me collected requires keeping my sleep *sacred*. Six to seven hours of silent worship under duvets, quilts, sheets, covers of all kinds. To sleep peacefully and restfully so I can keep my thoughts solid and my brain, that's prone to wander, in a place where it can't get too far.

Protect your *sleep* to protect yourself.

When sleep starts to slip through my fingers and rush in rivulets from my mind, I can feel the changes that start out subtle but promise to rage. At first, tired and foggy. Fuzzy head fueling irritability with sadness seeping in, leading to bleary eyes that see *nothing* but dizzy blurs. Wobbled anxiety coloring every thought and tainting every action, growing steadily more *misunderstood*.

Or just tired. Just feeling worn with thoughts that drag a bit. My body aching slightly and my mind all muddy and s l o w . Not sad, just cumbersome. But the occasional speck of bright shines through and I feel a quick jolt of tingled promise. And I wonder, how can I stroke this *fire*.

The irritable, bleary eyes struggle to close and find any sleep that counts. I cannot sleep, and this fact contributes to the dizziness and fuzziness as I fail to control my blurred world and a brain that sees tainted colors. I am sad and angry at a body that can't settle and a brain that will not sleep in the way I need it to.

The draggging cumbersome eyes start to experience more specks of sparkle that rip through me like red currents. I am tired at first and muddy at first, but with each electric shock, I start to see more clearly than I ever have before. This fire will keep me *clean* and *free* and I will be a me that does not need six to seven hours a night because I. am. complete.

I begin to rage with confusion. I feel out of control and angry with each distorted thought that I can't use in my life; telling me things that become more and more real because I have nothing else to hold on to. I am angry, scared, and crying with my whole body because the things I *know* are frightening and difficult to believe. But I have nothing else to hold on to. The world stops making sense and I realize that I. never. did.

The psychiatrist says
Mania with mixed episodes.

I tell him about my poisoned granola bar and my body full of glass,
Psychotic features.

My teeth fall out one by one and my fingers start unraveling. These are my worries.
These pills will protect you.

I am beauty. This is why we live our lives—to feel this amazing energy and to be enlightened by our own brilliance. Our own sheer hypnotic magic that fills us with so much joy that you think you could b u r s t—*into*—s t a r s. Who needs control? Who needs sleep? Who needs food? The only belief I need is in my crystal heart that reflects light—reflects my exquisitely crafted soul out into the world, showing everyone that this is what radiance looks like. I. am. here. I have no worries.

The psychiatrist says
*Hypomania with a guarantee of a dramatic, clinically quantifiable crash
and a depressive episode on the other side.
These pills will protect you.*

On the other side of my eyes, I listen to the whisperings of a mind that volleys between mania, hypomania, psychosis, depression, and the Rachel who sleeps well at night. Protect my sleep. Protect with pills. Balance the back and forth.

Temper the to and fro.

My brain is prone to wander to places too far from the quilt, where it seeks crumbling shelter in confused terror, or escapes into an awe-filled landscape of *e x p l o s i v e delight*.

Protect myself from the thoughts that tell me to let go.

Protect myself from the ends of this ill continuum.

in every color

I saw "god" scrawled across the walls in every color you can imagine, but the brush strokes wouldn't lay still. They dripped and they spilled, chaos you can't even fathom.

The paint stained the ceiling and floor, it was all black before, but now you see every shade in a cesspool of ink. My hands are covered in purples and greens, and I'm not who I seem, but the red, orange, and yellow on my tongue make you think.

You see me standing beneath the grey lights that grow ever darker each night, as my fingertips bleed blue hues on the concrete. My face may have its place, this freckle filled space, but it's not my smile that reminds you how often we meet.

Because your job is to write "god" to the tune of all the applause, across every surface that you can find. Script immortalized in black paint that silently drips, wilts, and faints, but lately, you've been losing your mind.

Because as soon as "god" is splashed like a brand by your eager hand, and you've left to find more blank spaces to preach, I appear the second you're gone, so quickly nobody knows something went wrong, and I smear paint everywhere I can reach.

You stencil "god" in dark black, but where's the fun in that, so I ruin your work with rainbows and rivers and monsoons. Oh, the magnitude of this mess, but I bet you can guess why I trade your word for a landscape of bursting balloons.

Because if god is actually real, I just know they would feel that they're more than letters that can easily be left behind, so I offer a rainbow drawn over your head, overflowing with colors instead, and it's so beautiful, we forget we're out of time.

the devious science of the psychosis slip-up

Missing the anti-psychosis dose, the dose I probably need the most,

brings sickness hard to fathom, only the true psychotic can imagine,

because as the medicine stops sinking in, the crazy thinking starts to begin,

and the loudest of my delirious wills demands I skip additional pills,

then the pattern of passing on prescriptions soon becomes my new addiction,

the psychotic tickle in my head says, *Don't take pills, be "you" instead,*

but this crazy "you" slips quicker and quicker,
and before you know it, you're sicker and sicker,

and then you're stricken, practically comatose,
and you tell yourself to take your goddamn dose.

active duty

I open up my medicine cabinet to a cylindrical psychiatric army.

Standing at attention, they eye me obediently.

See-through orange vials filled with capsules and pills,
they live to serve.

Some days, it's reassuring to see them all lined up,
their only purpose to keep my head on straight.

But other days, the endless rows are a sobering reminder of how crazy
I actually am to need so many reinforcements tucked away behind my mirror.

And then there are the times they mutiny and refuse to do their jobs,
so I grow crazier and crazier,

And while they may be stuffed to the cusp with piles of pills and topped off with
cotton, they might as well be empty because, by then, my brain is too far gone
for them to even make a difference.

Going AWOL.

There have been a few times when their mutiny morphs from willful
disobedience to violent revolt.

When each and every stack of tablets, innards and entrails peaking out at me
from transparent casings, mock me, court me, do whatever it takes to convince
me to swallow every last soldier and simply wait to die, to be free, to be better
and less of a burden.

Fucked up beyond all recognition.

But thankfully, most of the time, my battalion of orange bottles work together.
I pop off their lids and rattle the ranks,
and as each dose slides down my throat, I know that today I will be okay.

I can go out into the world at ease.

autopsy

"Let's perform an autopsy,"
said the psychiatrist in front of me.

I choked and stammered, "But I'm alive."
"Well, this seems like a great time to die."

He rolled up his sleeves and pushed me to the floor,
"I think your brain might be one I haven't seen before."

I struggled and strained as he sat on my chest,
and he clucked his tongue saying, "Sweetie, I know what's best."

He then forced his thick thumbs into my pleading, watery eyes.
He found my brain pink, wet, and wincing on the other side.

"Hmm," he smirked as he pinched, prodded, and poked.
He peeled away layers and folds, laughing like my brain made a joke.

I squirmed as he showed me his favorite bits of pale pink and grey.
He organized them in jars and bottles with labels for display.

I started crying blood and coughing up debris.
I tried to scream, but there was brain in my mouth, and I couldn't see.

I whimpered and wriggled, and he pinned me down with his fists,
"Hun, please be compliant while I finish all this."

He gestured to the sharp bits of skull that littered the floor.
With his toe, he kicked something and exclaimed, "I've never seen that before!"

"Your brain is rotting with trauma, you're bipolar and battered.
Let me carve a bit deeper to see what's really the matter."

He tore open my scalp and jammed his fingers inside,
and at that very moment, I knew I would die.

Pawing through my skull, his face suddenly turned from delight to disgust,
"Sigh. You're nothing new. Just another emotional woman making a fuss."

"With your insistent whining, you all bore me to death,"
he angrily grumbled and muttered, "What a waste," under his breath.

He rolled down his sleeves, ignoring the bits of gristle, blood, and bone,
and he turned to exit his office, leaving me ripped open and alone.

I wheezed out some words through my pink lips and red tongue,
"I'm going to tell everyone what you have done."

He let out a bellowing laugh and joyfully shook his head,
"Sweetheart, you can't say shit to anybody because you're fucking dead."

"Don't worry, I'll tell your friends and family what they always knew -
you finally killed yourself, something that they expected you'd do."

"Suicide makes perfect sense considering your brain, don't'cha think?
I'm the expert, I make the decisions, I'm in charge, I'm the shrink."

"No one will ask any questions, and they'll miss you for a while,
just as long as it takes me to mop all this useless gunk into a pile."

"Alright, lights out. It's time for you to close your eyes and drool until you're gone."
And I knew he was right, so I just went along.

I closed my eyes and let myself die,
because he was right - why should I bother, why should I even try?

It's a curse you can't lift, a game you can't win,
and when doctors and employers and family weigh in,

assumptions are made and these lies seem so true,
because being crazy is the only thing you'll ever do.

When I'm psychotic, *my teeth sprout weeds; bushes I can't chew my way out of.*

Dandelion chains tighten around my tongue.

Angry ivy latticework bridges the ceiling of my mouth.

Spores swing from my eyelids.

Sap coats my sticky, swollen lower lip.

When I ask for help, my voice is lost under the rattling of thistles that crowd my throat.

How can I take medication that promises to kill my garden?

our roots

Stealing our fingertips,
filleting each tender pad from each fleshy stump,
gluing this soft slice of skin discreetly upon the swaying leaves of a red-handed tree,
our unique nothingness caught in spiraling climber vines,
which will eventually collect the rest of us,
sifting through our tissue and bones when we finally die in the ground,
giving our mortal meat to the trees

carnivorous

Embedded in my subterranean jaw is an extra molar.

And it is growing like a tumor, barreling its way to the surface of my mouth, all because it wants a taste.

I'm worried it will take the wrong tunnel and shoot out of the back of my head, spiraling into the stale air, a rogue molar leaving a loose wound behind my ear.

My skin around the exit gash flapping in the breeze it leaves as it ricochets out into the city.

Droplets of blood flicked onto my collar as the molar finds something better.

I am left toothless, stuck wearing a rotten hole.

being in my skin

I am nothing but ripe skin. Fresh pale skin tugged at the seams as it promises to cover and connect every single sliver of my freckled pieces of person. Tiny hairs march across my body and hold hands as they clomp across the crowded pathway of my person. Scars that are pink and white and raw and aged, tied to memories of sadness felt in the sobbing cavity of my chest, nestled in the skeleton-cage of my person. Protruding nails from keratin armies that are nibbled and gnawed into practically nothing but nubs that throb and fester on my person. Crooked teeth with caps and chips that guide you through plaque and decaying streets of mouth with a tongue laying limp in the middle of town that finally gave up trying to see through parted pink, rough lips. And my eyes do nothing but lie. I am skin.

some kind of silence

Whispers through the wallpaper.

Plaster cracking in the hollow of your throats.

I hear whistles like breathy words. Like bird languages, long and quick, like my husband telling the dogs to come inside.

But the drumming hum keeps coming, telling me to start making quilts for captives, adorned with pebbles and winks.

Craft cradles for babies with too-tired eyes who choose not to cry anymore.

The innermost whistles pressing against wooden panels won't wake up the neighbors, but I hear them murmur through the marrow in my bones.

Pushing through the sick, syrupy plasma, thick and hesitant to echo for anyone but me.

The wild eyes on the other side of the wall, through winks and through blinks, say I make cradles for nothing because I am just crazy.

And the squint-worthy words tell me to forget to see stars.

I thought madness was done with this next mouthful of medication, but the walls seethe and creep, pushing pus and crammed wails through their sutures.

I click my tongue as I sit and I ache, staying still and praying for some kind of silence.

I am scared and full of noises that no one else hears.

I tilt my head, trying to capture the sirens, and whistle to the babies who choose to not open their eyes anymore.

And I desperately want to stitch together blankets of wallpaper and skin for the creatures caught in my mind.

But instead, I close my eyes viciously, and I grip my shoulders violently, and I rock, and I try to block out the din of the dying, but I can't fall asleep because I am too crazy to be tucked in.

So, I swallow my fist, and I sift through my tears, and I wait and I wonder when the voices will stop teaching me how to be lonely enough to die.

the color of dying

Are we alive only to kill each other?

Does Jesus keep a tally of how many souls he receives? It feels like the end end end end of the universe.

He must be tired of counting.

I cry so often these days because there are so many reasons to rip out your stitches. There is more evidence of sadness and violence and grieving and torture and hatred than the happiness and tenderness and compassion and peace and love that used to radiate from the now burned out lightbulbs above us us us us.

We are in the darkness.

The only particles of light we can grasp are used to find people weaker than ourselves to brutalize, to kill, and then add the dead to Jesus's seemingly never-ending receipt. He buys us back one by one by one by one as we die die die die and he wishes he had never helped make us. He prays to the other parts of his heart, the God and Holy Ghosts on his shoulders, but they can't give him any answers.

This is me, and I don't believe in Jesus. But if I did believe, this is how he would explain this human mess to me: He would smile softly and hold my hand. His whispers would send pirouettes of quiet, calming crimson light into my eyes. He would wrap his warm arms around my brittle bones. He would be so completely, all consumingly gentle that I would forget how to exist exist exist exist. But he would never answer my questions, just cluck his tongue and tame my wild hair.

Jesus is not a part of me or a part of this world. Jesus is not real. But my Diana is. My Princess Diana has always cradled me in long lace-gloved forearms. She swaddles me so tightly and keeps me safe with her elegance and crystal eyes. Her gaze tirelessly reassuring and peaceful and oh-so-ultraviolet, you can see it even when all the bulbs have broken. Lavender light light light light steeped in hopeful dreams.

My Diana is real.

She is supposed to be real, but finding her is harder now. When she tries to find me, she drowns in the escalating number of deaths scrawled out in angry, bubbled blood by Jesus's own hand. He pricked four fingertips with his crown of thorns and drew bright red blood to ink out suicide notes for families that cry cry cry cry in the dark dark dark dark, just like me. I cry for my Princess Diana who wears a tiara of brightness decorated with beams of heather-tainted light and dotted with luminous stars, emblems of safety and everything I used to hold on to for hope. Now she suffocates under the staggering weight of her diadems, entwined with too much disease.

This is me me me me.

I can't help but see that Jesus is weak from bloodletting, and that my Diana can't get to me because she has been swept away in this red, remorseful river. Humanity is dying, and some of us cry and some of us try to love love love love but others just shoot shoot shoot shoot until we are all heavy with death and washed away.

Blackness and empty arms.

I miss being held. Miss miss miss miss.

Is this the color of dying?

distracted as i die

Bipolar disorder keeps me distracted as I die.
I entice it with sweet lies and soft deceit, and then it's too late.
Fingertips as petals on the bed, eyeballs smeared across the ceiling.
I lie down just to look at myself and I smile at the bones.
My consciousness spirals out into space.
I would laugh except she's got me by the throat.
So, I choke and coo and cuddle her palms with my cheeks as she untethers my spine.
Serene sick nothingness leaking into the celestial wasteland.
A break from disease.
A peaceful nonexistence.
My husband weeps as he carves an epitaph with my teeth.
"Here lies my love, so much more than this disorder."
But I'm not paying attention.

When I slit my wrists twelve years ago, I wonder what sound I made.

While everything else is vivid, permanently branded in my brain, I can't play back the sounds that accompanied my almost-suicide. All there is are echoes trapped inside my ears.

What happened in the background as I pressed razor to wrist?
Did I gasp with the puncture? Did I whimper or moan?

I remember the searing sting of filleted skin.
I remember my left hand quivering under the cut, my right hand barely flinching.
My arms turned from pale to pink to pale again, and the blood turned from bright to black to red to stains on the carpet.

I remember how at first the incision felt good, tasting like metal under my tongue.
The cut was deep and raw and electric, like a tart pinch in the chewed-up cavity of my cheek.
I remember the pain feeling like sex, a jolt that made me think about God, my eyes growing as wide as the sky above my ceiling.

Did I suck in my breath quickly and tightly? Scraping air through my crooked teeth?
I bet my heart raced and my face flushed.
I wonder how hard my shoulders shook.

I remember blinking blood and breathing pinched pain and, for a split second, as my skin started slipping apart, it felt like an awakening.

The pain made my vision clear and my senses alive with fire.

God called for me to come home.

I remember my eyes tearing up because I was so happy and sad all at once because I was about to die. Tears sliding down my nose, leaving hot, salted, shimmering ribbons laced across my freckled skin.

Did I exhale with a loud sigh of relief? Of exasperation? Of desperation?

What was said that day?

I remember crying because I was CRAZY and I had no choice.

I remember calling the god tethered in my skull, he who has no need for words or language, who with grief and shame and anger batters my brain into submission.

I remember crying even harder because he didn't care about me after all.

Did I cry out? Call out to anyone?

Did I tell anyone goodbye?

Did I tell myself things would be better now?

Did I believe it?

Or was I silent?

I still wonder if my skin whispered when it was sliced open.

If it made a hissing noise like a carved, red snake.

If the wound gurgled or audibly wept like my eyes did.

If I murmured reassuringly under the loudness of my decision that this was for the best.

I wonder if the smeared blood muted the sound of fingers sliding across my forearms, fingering the incisions?

What was the soundtrack of my almost-suicide?
A reel of memories with no volume.
I just can't remember the last words of my body.
Even though they are always on the tip of my tongue.

When I become bipolar in my palace and barricaded by my madness,
I routinely act astonished, declaring that *this wasn't how I planned it.*

I grow desperate in this depression, and I lose track of all my days,
and I feel lost in loneliness and exhaustion because I can't subsist in haze.

In a prison made of turrets wrapped in wire watchtowers with no eyes,
I can still see what's going on around me but can't feel the bits of life outside.

Trapped in anxiety and worthlessness, I forget that I'm strong and smart,
and that I have the key to spring the latches that snare and squeeze my heart.

But when I linger in my agony, this psychotic castle shows its face,
and I'm locked inside a decrepit hovel, my keys perpetually misplaced.

And then this shack of misery entombs me, until I lose myself to fatal sick,
because I always, always ask for quarantine that I built with my own bricks.

dark dreams
of being in the labyrinth

"I don't feel like I'm in my body, but I don't feel like I'm anywhere else,"
said the creature crawling around the cabinet on the highest fucking shelf.

And he sat behind the shutters of my very open skull,
and he whimpered and he puzzled why I stayed indoors at all.

Hanging from decaying twinkle lights with busted bulbs and dimming sparks,
the little morsel of a monster cackled that she preferred the dark.

So the clouds of scurrying premonitions, finding new places to duck and hide,
stay champions of the darkness, taking my fleshy, scratchy body for a ride.

Lounging in the hollows of a rib cage and a tired empty lung,
the macabre puppet party has only just begun.

And they dance inside my temples and look outward from my inward eyes,
and they tell me that it's their turn now and to let my human impulse die.

recurring

Piles of eyelids cling to castles in Madrid, I sigh as I sit in my cluttered cage.

Turreted beauty takes us all for a spin while our blinking is sorely delayed.

You see me and feel pity and invite me to dance because you think I am lost and alone,

but I turn and see you and the burden of your world, and my gaze turns your flesh into stone.

sow

I can hear it.

It's not a soft, slow motion exhale. It's not a crashing thud followed by rumbling. It's not fizzing or popping. It's not cracking or flooding.

No gushing, no rushing, nothing fevered. Nothing too alarming. Nothing too jarring. No broken glass. No toppled street hydrant. No speeding train. At least not right away.

A wet bulb. That's how I start.

My brain is a healthy, wet bulb that glistens with residue. With water and earth, it's slick to touch and twinkles when you twist it in your fingers. You can barely hear me grow. My brain is a bulb slowly wrestled from the soil.

Earnest but broken, roots trail from my base, and I am squeaky damp in the sunlight. I anchor myself between thumb and forefinger and rub my wet, slick skin like a worry stone. The moisture sighs under my nails.

But soon, I strike, faster and faster. I can't escape as I rub my skull in concentric circles. I start to erase myself with determined rhythm. Massaged away by precise, persistent touching.

I can't stop.

You can hear my roots starting to wail. They flake off in stringy dirt clumps as I continue to shed layers of thin white skin.

I start sloughing off cells and sweet water. My bulb crushed under my anxious thumbprint, peeled apart, piece by piece, my mind dripping onto the floor. The droplets methodically boring holes in my brain, becoming ravenous torrents, until I run dry and my head is left barren.

I am nothing but the vibrations of madness. A leftover echo of raw fingers with nothing left to tease. From silent murmurs to angry cascades, you see me transform. Healthy, quiet wetness until my brain battens down the hatches and all I do is watch as I thunder and wring myself dry.

Rip my roots right from the soaked earth.

I stab stubby fingers into my skull, a bulb smashed between greedy hands. I'm pulp and gristle. Gagged and rattled. I'm tired and tortured. Pulverized into merciless pieces.

A brain once protected under the soil now exposed and ridiculed. I scorch and salt the pink jelly congealed behind my eyes. It sounds like resigned crying.

To me, crazy isn't a weed. It's my next breath. It's my life. I lose it again and again. Yet somehow, I still smile noiselessly as dry dust cracks in the corners of my lips.

counterclaim

plausible sanity, you've got to hand it to me, even at my craziest i can act like i am sane,

and the weirdest thing about it is that the infection in my brain

is growing increasingly fevered as my grey matter tugs and strains

the wicked, wild side of this illness is that i'm suddenly 100% deranged,

yet the performance i am giving could land me a supernova on the walk of fame

because, despite the fact that i'm sick and losing it and my brain's a heavy, crazy stain,

the doctors are impressed at the healthy façade that i can feign,

the truth is it's simply easier to go psychotic and stuff my eyeballs down the drain,

so i scream louder and louder and louder because madness is my heart's refrain,

and i grind my teeth and rip out my hair because i'm the only one to blame,

by the end, i've peeled off all my freckles and i know i'll never be the same,

it's tricky being mentally ill when you can act like your mind is compliant and tame

when, in reality, you're cracked, diseased, and dying, and isn't that a fucking shame

off

My mind is so electric that I'm turning on all the traffic lights,
crackling and cackling, my brain is wired completely wrong.
It flickers and blinks, it fizzles and spits.
I'm short-circuiting and scintillating, but my incandescence isn't making any sense.
My husband can't fall asleep when my eyeballs are generating such bright light,
but I can't close my eyes while lying in bed or else I'll sizzle off my eyelids.

I wish I could make it stop.

The top story of my two-story brick house is glowing, glistening, and pulsing.
People can see me seething from the street.
They complain about the festering white lights,
but I'm at the mercy of a mind that won't turn off
It's a miracle that I can still light up the sky after so many wild nights, after so many sedatives
and so much sickness, after so many years with a brain that must be turning black by now.

I wish I could slow down.

I cough up bits of shiny brain and hold the jelly in my creased palms,
viscous pink goo that quivers and smells like dying skin,
I stick colored candles into the mushy mounds and they ignite.
My fists oozing with flickering candlelight and gelatinous remains,
my fingertips burn off with every stutter and stumble.

I wish there was another way.

I hear the hissing behind my ears and smell the smoke seeping from my mouth.
My tongue is charred at the anchor where meat meets throat, and singed at the tip where

my pink pointed tongue drums against my flint-like teeth.
The sparks keep me smiling and my lips bleeding.
I am always falling apart.
I am always crying out for help.
I am infinite, drooling entropy.

I wish this wasn't me.

plot

One of these days, I'll remove my own brain,
wipe away the blood and peel off the cellophane.
I'll be kind to my brain and raise it as my own,
I'll let it play on my lawn and live in my home.
I'll push my brain on a swing and tuck it in at night,
I'll pat its pulpy mush and sing songs when I turn out the light.
I'll help my brain tie its shoes so it doesn't trip over its feet,
I'll hold my brain's hand as we walk side by side down the street.
I'll kiss my brain's boo-boos when it stumbles and falls,
I'll let it hang One Direction posters all over its bedroom walls.
I'll help my brain with its homework and college applications,
I'll support my brain's decisions and uphold high expectations.
I'll save for a wedding and help my brain by a house,
I'll smile in all the photos and get along with its spouse.

But one of these nights, I'll pop by, pretending to give it my best,
and from out of nowhere, I'll grab it by the throat and stab my finger in its chest.
I'll throw my brain down the stairs and I'll dig out each eye,
I'll tell it my love has always been a lie.
I'll cut out its tongue and I'll smash in its teeth,
it will gurgle and plead, struggling from beneath.
I'll laugh as it drools and I'll sever its arms and its legs,

it'll whisper and weep and look pathetic as it begs.
My brain will stare into my eyes, shudder, shake, and ask why,
and I'll tell it one last story as I watch it slowly die.
Because even though I played nice with my brain for awhile,
hidden behind every methodical laugh, every saccharine smile,
I've always hated this pink piece of shit that's lived in my head.
It got sick when I was fifteen, and since then, I've wished it was dead.

Why would I ever live with a brain who ruined my life,
when I could lure it into love and then dissect it with a knife?
Don't fuck with me brain, I see you for what you truly are,
a glistening wad of garbage wrapped in madness and tar.
So I'll strangle my brain and laugh long and hard into the night,
and the newspapers will be baffled, saying everything seemed alright.
I'll walk calmly from the house in handcuffs and wink at the press,
and I'll turn to the journalists to give my last address,
because I know I'll get the chair and I'm ready to die,
but I want to answer when they inevitably ask me "Why?"
I killed my brain because all it ever wanted was to kill me,
I always knew this to be true, given the right opportunity.
So I tricked it into living my life, keeping my enemy close,
and I was patient and calculating and meticulous, goodness knows.
And then the day was right, and well, you saw the remains,
and I'm the happiest I've ever been because now I don't have a brain.

aftershock

Symptomatic for the past week and a half and I'm finally cresting sanity. When you're coming out of a manic or depressive episode, you have to follow your individualized mental illness protocol to climb and clamor your way back to normalcy. You survey the damage to see what you've done and what you need to do in order to re-enter the real world.

I eye the evidence left on my arm, scratches and tiny slits. Sometimes I cut when I'm psychotic and I just can't breathe. I start suffocating, choking on fear and illness, and I guess the slicing works, because I'm still standing, breathing, just with a quietly nicked forearm. The red, angry tears are a distraction from wanting to die. Those cuts can keep me from killing myself because they remind me that I'm real, not just delusions packaged in the shape of a person. In case of emergency, break skin, I guess.

I embark on a scavenger hunt for missing items, like used glasses and office supplies. It's actually the easiest game ever. Crazy-me leaves sane-me clues all over the house. I find cups and mugs all over the place, clouded with fingerprint smudges and imprints of kissed lips. Very rarely is there leftover water or juice or milk or whatever could have taken up residence in the bottom of the cup because I've turned them all upside down. Otherwise, I would have just been asking to be poisoned, said paranoid-me. My ill self is never bothered with the dishes because she dedicates all of her energy and effort on escaping a poisonous death. I stock the dishwasher with mugs and recycle plastic cups only when I start to realize that I'm not saving my life, I'm just making a mess.

Similarly, I find paperclips and pens and pencils in the cracks and crevices of my furniture. When I'm cycling, they seem overwhelming and ominous. They watch everything I do. I've planted binder clips under the mattress and loose staples collect on my windowsill. I find a staple remover with pointed fangs in the bottom of my closet, imprisoned under a pile of dirty clothes. A dismembered tape dispenser wedged underneath the leg of my desk. My desk is cockeyed, but what matters is I'm okay. This is me, crazy - I have to hunt down, police, bury, and dissect these instruments that are no doubt reporting on me to some unseen spy conglomerate that wants to take over the world. One tack at a time. But luckily, I'm sane now, so I collect my no longer insidious, infiltrating stash of school supplies because I need to get back to work.

I try to convince myself that I am not useless. And this last step is the most challenging of all. Forcing myself to believe that I should not be embarrassed of this disorder. That it is okay to let work sit aside for a week or so, or more, because sick-me just can't do it, even if the healthy-me cries out to be productive. It is still hard to return to the world and say, "I was busy being mentally ill, but now I'm back." I'm ashamed of all of it.

I pray that no one asks me about the bizarre details of the last two weeks because I know that the truth will make everyone uncomfortable. I worry that if people really knew, they wouldn't want to stick around; to wait for me to put my head on straight. For me to twist and turn my skull in place so my mind doesn't topple to the floor and shatter. I tell myself that feeling guilty and being secretive is a waste of my energy. I remind myself that illness isn't a moral failing. That talking about falling apart dismantles stigma. But it's hard. My expectations are all over the place. I can be an advocate for others who struggle with mental illness, I can be the picture perfect case study of a career crazy person. But in the same breath, I denounce myself and dismiss my value because I just can't shake this feeling of worthlessness and disgust because I let illness run my life. It's a lot to live up to.

This is my bipolar aftershock. Evidence of what happened in my brain played out as quirky madness throughout my house. Conversations with myself to work through the pangs of self-loathing. Things that I have to try to understand and deal with during the days after. I struggle to sort through it and slide back into my routine. But I do it. I clean the cuts and find the cups. I send myself little love letters, *"I can do it!"* and sweep safety pins from under the bed. This is the bipolar debris that I need to pick up and put back on the right shelves. After an episode, this is how I get back to life. I can do it, I've done it before, and I know I'll have to do it for years to come. I think it gets easier, even with the realization that I keep getting sicker. Ultimately, I'm in charge.

FOUR

depression

mental illness
in four acts

i have bipolar disorder, but I didn't always call it that.

When I was fifteen, I first became aware of how my body and brain didn't always work quite right. Because sometimes, I would suddenly become enveloped in a sparkly, colorful, and beautiful swell of euphoria that saved me and swallowed me whole. I later learned to call this act "hypomania," but I didn't need words back then. I just needed to hold on to this deliriously intoxicating invincibility.

I was only introduced to the name "bipolar" when I was seventeen and I felt out of control, agitated, lost, and so overwhelmingly blurry that I was taken to the first of many psychiatrists. I was diagnosed, and the doctor told me this act is "mania."

At nineteen, I learned the phrase "mania with psychotic features" when I capsized under the raging torrent of this illness as it obstructed and disrupted my everyday life. I learned to pair that feeling with that name while on the inpatient unit. Psychosis felt like I was on fire and cracking erratically into fragments.

ACT ONE: hypomania, ACT TWO: mania, ACT THREE: psychosis.

But when did I first feel depression? ACT FOUR: depression. I've never been in love with, morbidly curious about, or as scared of that state, so I always forget ACT FOUR. I forget until it is too late and I feel nothing but its aching hopelessness and I wonder if I will feel this way forever. Or maybe I always feel this way but I am just too easily sidetracked waiting for acts one through three. Living acts one through three. Acting out acts one through three. ACT FOUR robs me of all momentum as I suffocate in the numbness and the nothing that we all call "depression" - a name and feelings I want to forget and never feel again.

mania center stage: myself as the understudy

"What exactly happened that brought you here today?" Dr. V asked from his large leather recliner, peering down at my mother and me swaying on our fraying wicker seats. Behind him was a wall-sized photograph of the Taj Mahal, plastered on the right hand corner of which, next to a poorly pixelated column, was a picture of a yellow rubber ducky. I would've sworn I was hallucinating. It was the strangest backdrop for a psychiatrist's office, but my mother saw it too and was equally confused. Dr. V was the answer to our prayers - the primary prayer being an answer to the question, "Why is Rachel crazy?" and the secondary prayer was that he could give us the cure. And even though I was hating every minute of this visit, sitting there, riddled with self-loathing, embarrassment, and shame, I was glad the doctor had asked that question because I wanted to know, too. I had done a lot of crazy things, especially since turning seventeen. Which was the one that tipped my parents' concern? Was it the secret long walks I felt compelled to take in the middle of the night? The crooked cuts that appeared on my legs - so many now that they were difficult to hide? The fact I smoked weed once in awhile, sipped vodka occasionally, or took someone else's prescription pills? Maybe it was my clandestine and bizarre attraction to Princess Diana, which had developed for unknown reasons. I crossed my fingers, hoping I would not have to explain that last one.

"She thought she was on a TV show," sighed my mom.

I will never forget that face. That look of worry and love all jumbled together too complexly that I could never distill one from the other ever again. The day I realized my mom would forever love me with worry in her eyes was the day I realized my TV show was officially going off the air.

Okay, so I launched my own TV show. No big deal. I grew up in a household that adored female talk show hosts, from Rosie O'Donnell to Oprah Winfrey, to Ellen DeGeneres in later years. These strong, smart women had overcome adversity—they were pioneers of feminism on television, they were engaging and entertaining, they made people laugh, and they were role models to all of us. It didn't take a genius to realize that this was a path worth pursuing. Luckily, I was a genius, so I decided to make it happen. I would start small but eventually change lives on prime time television.

"Dad, what kinds of peas are these?" I asked my father one night at dinner during a live taping.

"I don't know. Green! I thought you liked peas?"

"I do, but I need to know the brand."

"Why do you need to know the brand?"

"Because if I don't know, how will everyone else!?"

Uh oh. In that moment, the *"Rach, you can be so quirky"*-look I had grown accustomed to seeing on my parents' faces was replaced with furrowed brows and pensive stares. I had only wanted to rave about the peas for my dedicated audience so they could buy the exact same kind and reap all the same nutritional benefits that I was consuming at the Kallem family dinner. But when I said it all out loud, I realized that it sounded crazy. I sounded crazy. It had made so much sense before and I believed it with all my heart. Having a studio audience made me feel real and purposeful in a way I had never felt before. It finally felt like I fit. After being haunted for months by the unsettling feeling that people might be watching me, the enraptured fans tuning in now were my welcomed guests.

But with a thunderous roar reverberating in my head, so loud it drowned out the audience's applause, my completely-real-to-me architectured world came crashing down with the realization that I must be crazy. I was crazy, stupid, and shatteringly devastated. I hoped no one would take serious notice of this cognitive transgression and, in utter disgrace, I put the writers on hiatus and dug my slightly rusted scissors out of my dresser drawer, fully aware that I was back to collecting cuts and raiding medicine cabinets. Unfortunately, my parents noticed, and since I was nowhere near as mesmeric as Oprah, I never met a casting agent or an interested executive. Instead, I met with Dr. V, the man who would be my psychiatrist. At our visit, he told me I had bipolar I disorder and needed to take medication for the foreseeable future.

You've got to be rubber ducking kidding me. Not only was I an insecure, overweight teenager, and a failed aspiring talk show personality, but now I was also certifiably insane. A long ongoing list of my erratic behaviors was filed in my psychiatrist's office, and all I wanted was to be normal like everyone else. The worst part of it all, though, was that I've always hated peas with a passion.

If you want to grossly simplify it, bipolar disorder is all about alternating moods. Except these moods, or emotional states, are extremely heightened versions of the feelings most of us experience every day. My cycling emotional states were classified as hypomania (the fun Rachel who I think everyone adores), mania (the high energy, do-it-all Rachel who doesn't notice the quizzical looks), psychosis (the Rachel who is torn apart by terror that no one else can see or understand), and depression (the Rachel who can't bear it any longer).

Dr. V prescribed me a long list of pills that promised to take away the ache and help me manage my symptoms, but the combination of capsules and tablets left my brain feeling damp and foggy. My thoughts became too thick to think and, worst of all, my hypomania and mania, who had made me feel so light, sparkly, and TV-worthy, all but disappeared under the weight of these mood stabilizers and antipsychotics. Losing hypomania and mania felt like losing the best parts of myself. I figured I was miserable either way, so why should I forfeit the one thing that made me happy? Holding firm with this rationale, I flushed my medications down the toilet and resolved to make things better on my own. I had willpower and discipline. I could do it. (I extend my sincerest apologies to the highly mellowed out fish I inadvertently sedated in the Chesapeake Bay.)

Despite my parents' concerns, after graduating from high school, I attended college about two hours away from home, which is where I first tasted how sweet life could be with minimal adult supervision. In my newfound collegiate freedom, mania truly shined. She became the beacon of light in the Sisyphean cycling of my illness. Mania blessed me with electric emotions, erotic ideas, and brilliant behaviors, which while they may have been clinically considered symptoms of my sickness, were divinely exalting for me. She gave me the confidence and carelessness to channel the diva I always hoped I was and emboldened me to do whatever I wanted. *Why not?* I was marvelous, sublime, and lust-worthy.

The psychosis and depression always loomed, so I enjoyed the mania while I could. Thankfully, college made that pretty doable seeing as I could easily schedule my daily agenda around my mania. Her never-ending energy and outright refusal to recognize that the real world has consequences enabled me to stay up all night, eat next to nothing, bask in the glittering glow of my own perfection, and, for as long as I could, I harnessed my mania to keep myself in motion. Something definitely felt off, but my parents cautiously accepted that I must be "okay." My grades were good, I saw my therapist and psychiatrist regularly, and I called home every week. But were things "okay?" No. Leading this double life - a crazy party girl masquerading as a sane model citizen - placed so much pressure on my brain that, unbeknownst to me, I began to splinter.

My drug of choice was particularly potent and highly volatile. It comes highly individualized, tailored to meet the exact needs of each addict. It speaks to you so personally and reads you so accurately that it is nearly impossible to turn down. I liken the special effects of my personal batch to exuberant fireworks whizzing and popping in my skull. When I'm submerged in its aura, everything is electric and I am a beautiful, unpredictable livewire. *How can I possibly say no to this feeling?* Especially considering I get it for free. I cook up this magnetic high in my own cranial chemistry set, and thus, it is beyond easy to slip into this shameless, hazardous addiction. I willingly take the euphoria, the invincibility, and the immortality that leaves me feeling completely divine.

At seventeen, when I was diagnosed with bipolar disorder, my hypomania was alluring and intoxicating. However, in the whirlwind that was college, my hypomania rocketed from a somewhat manageable blissful state to full blown mania. Mania brought miraculous feelings, sensations, realizations, and abilities that I never knew I had. Mania and I truly made for a stunning pair. I think somewhere in the back of my mind, I always knew she would eventually kill me, but, oh, what a majestic, spectacular death it would be.

I once spent 72 hours, the weekend before midterms my junior year of college, researching the most notorious serial killers in the history of the United States. Taken at face value, someone reading about the gruesome crimes of John Wayne Gacy, Ted Bundy, Jeffrey Dahmer, and Aileen Wuornos is morbid and macabre, but many people share a psychological fascination about infamous mass murderers. And most college students succumb to the sweet siren song of procrastination. However, after hours of intensive nonstop research, Googling related horror stories, surfing sinister Wikipedia pages, and watching chilling YouTube videos, I became incredibly paranoid, fearing for my life, and I didn't sleep much for almost two weeks.

I was so stricken with anxiety and tormented by the seemingly very real fear that someone was trying to poison me that I only ate packaged food for two months. *But a college student living on cheap, packaged food seems kinda normal, right?* I could feel the rusted corners of my brain turn to clotted dust, but I thought from the outside looking in I was a convincing college student. *I could keep this up.*

The summer before my senior year of college, I intellectualized my ingenious investment strategy of funneling my parent provided allowance into the George Foreman Grill market. No one in their right mind needs eight George Foreman Grills, but I was just pretending to be " right," so it seemed like a brilliant way to "spend money to make money." The logic was certifiably sound, at least to me. Will George Foreman Grills ever be recognized as legitimate currency? Hell no. Do George Foreman Grills depreciate in value over time? Hell yes. They're just novelty infomercial gadgets. But when I purchased all eight, I honestly felt like I was planning wisely for my future. It took almost six years to pawn off all of those grills, but I was twenty, had my dad's credit card, and while it was ill-advised and kooky, no one was hurt. Not even my credit score. It seemed sane-ish.

But it is terrifying to lose yourself to an illness that courts you one minute and buries you the next. The times I've been admitted to the hospital, my psychosis was controlling me like a rattled puppet and I saw scrapes and scars on everyone and in every mirror and my eyes felt devilishly unfamiliar. I was frantic and terrified because nothing was real. And then, suddenly, in the very next moment, everything was too real and it was really bad. People were trying to poison me and trick me into killing myself. I couldn't see them and no one else could either but I just KNEW they were tucked behind every corner, dodging behind every shadow when I whipped my head around. I thought about God and Jesus and Princess Diana and how my teeth had betrayed me with their hidden microphones carved into yellowing enamel and their speakers glued to the underbelly of my tongue. And it was just hard to think straight and steady a thought long enough to make sense of it before it whizzed away and sparked, lighting a tiny fire in the corner of my mind that eventually raged and roared and left my head engulfed in wildfire. My brain was a bonfire. I was psychotic and all alone, abandoned in an inpatient unit. *Where was my intoxicating mania now?*

"I love you." The first time he said it, we had only been dating three months. Visiting my parents' home, canoodling in my childhood bed, propped on his elbow, his eyes cast on my face, he said, "Maybe it's too soon to say this, but I love you." My old bedroom built into the second floor of a typical suburban house has periwinkle wallpaper and glow-in-the-dark neon stars plastered erratically across four walls and the ceiling. That night, the room was radiating soft neon light like always, but I was tucked in bed with a warm body that was keeping my cold self safe and cozy. I beamed and told him I loved him, too, as I traced my fingers across the faint scar decorating his lower lip. He slipped playing Power Ranger tag when he was ten. It took me some time to share the stories behind my scars, but when I did, he listened patiently, held me close, and loved me wholeheartedly. We fell in love, madly and deeply, as twenty-year-olds do, and drunk on trust, I told him everything about myself, my disease, and the dark feelings that festered in my stomach.

The honesty and openness was liberating, and the fact he accepted me made me rethink how I felt about myself. Spencer helped me transform shame and silence into love and understanding. We went to different universities in different states but we spoke on the phone every night. I was a senior in college and I hadn't taken my medication in years. Orange prescription bottles lined the circumference of my bedroom floor, still stuffed with pills and topped off with cotton. I had to keep refilling my medications because if I didn't my parents would know I was going off the sanity grid.

Three months after our camp out in my childhood bedroom, he said, "I can help you, Rach, but you have to want this. You need to make this decision." Spencer's voice was eager yet supportive over the phone. I clutched my old Nokia that was crammed into a slightly too-small white plastic case dotted with cherries, and my confidence faltered for a second. My left hand was filled with the magic number of pills that promised to bring me back into myself, but I wasn't sure who that Rachel would be. Part of me was convinced I wouldn't love her and no one else would either. Back to a body marred with immeasurable flaws and inexcusable fatness. Reunited with a tattered heart, destined for loneliness and a malfunctioning brain that would make anyone embarrassed. All of this stuffed inside the sullen frame of an insecure teenager who was desperate to be normal. At that moment, I wasn't sure who the real me would be, but I knew bipolar and my dear friend mania were no replacement for a real relationship. They are not human. I knew for certain I loved him more than I loved mania. But I didn't think I loved myself enough.

Mania, with her effervescent sparkles, her complete lack of doubt, her polished charm and tantalizing charisma, helped me discover a body so beautiful that it deserved to love and be loved without apologizing or second guessing. Mania gifted me with treasured feelings of unparalleled excellence, cosmic importance, and incomparable brilliance. With her, I wasn't normal, I was extraordinary. But I was a danger to myself. The sobering truth I had successfully denied since I was seventeen soon became harder and harder to ignore, especially after stints in the psych unit. While my mania felt magical, opulent, and worthwhile, it had a deadly expiration date. Mania was deliciously otherworldly, up until I was catapulted into the terrifying atmosphere of psychosis, only to be viciously plunged into the murky depths of depression. Mania made me feel electrically alive but at the risk of hospitalization or even death. *Was it worth it? Was I worth it?*

I fingered the chalky pills in my palm that the FDA pledged would patch me up, but I had never given a chance before. These pills would end my love affair with mania, snuffing out her hypnotic open-all-night neon light. I wanted to fall in love with the boy on the other end of the phone who wasn't my savior but who could quite possibly be my soulmate. I whispered to myself a soft and scared, "You can do this." For the first time in my life, I decided I had to try and love myself without mania's candlelight vigil. And before I could change my mind, with one swift movement, I popped six pills in my mouth and drowned them with a glass of water. They left an unpleasant aftertaste on my tongue. I pressed my cell phone against my cheek and stated, "I can do this." I was really going to try this time.

I haven't seen the inside of a psychiatric ward since I was twenty-two because I refuse to let mental illness become my life. Yes, my life is much more "boring" now, but that's because when it comes to managing a mental illness the every day details are far from exciting or sensational. My self-care may look like trivial routines, monotonous habits, and meticulous patterns woven into every day life, but this gritty hard work is the lifeblood of taking your life back.

I don't want to be sick.

Hypomania, mania, psychosis, and depression are all parts of the same serious illness that tells you, you are worthless; parts that antagonize your anxiety, prey on the darkest fears tucked in your heart, and escalate your deterioration until Princess Diana is the only guardian angel you understand. I can't have mania in isolation. It is a package deal, which is why bipolar disorder is not a divine gift, it is an illness.

And I am not a diagnosis.

I finally understand that I have a mental illness, and I will always have it. And while that isn't "okay," it is my reality and I accept it. But that doesn't mean I only exist as a bipolar person. On the contrary, this is my life and I don't let bipolar disorder make my decisions anymore. I love the strong woman who lives at the center of each episode, who never leaves because she knows it gets better. I love the empowered woman who responsibly owns her mental illness so it begins to disrupt her life less and less.

I love myself. I'm better when I'm not sick.

I am carving out a future that is defined on my own terms based on the decisions I make every day. My future is bumpy yet bright.

Even without my George Foreman Grill fortune.

the real me

When I'm manic, I'm so **AMAZING** that I'm a shit to everyone else.
When I'm depressed, I lock myself inside because **I fucking hate myself.**
When I'm psychotic, **I'm on fire** and my teeth keep tearing me apart.
When I'm hypomanic, *life is blissful,* but that's **where the problems start.**
And after all the explosive cycling settles and my moods finally decide to subside,
I'm left here all alone as "Rachel," buried, depleted, ashamed, and completely fried.

i am a
good bipolar

I am a good bipolar.

I am a watchful bipolar.

I research myself every day.

In order to manage mental illness, you need to recognize the triggers and the tells that alert you to the fact that you're not-so-slowly inching away from sanity.

As those with mental illness know, there are some actions that universally signal that we're moments away from sinking into nothingness or setting ourselves on fire.

Not sleeping, sleeping too much, not eating, eating too much, never leaving your house, going out all night every night, all the drugs, all the drinking, all the money spent on all the dumbest things, making bad decisions, or doing nothing at all.

These can be easier to spot.

But in addition to that, we all have little things - little bizarre behaviors and skewed logic, little inklings unique to us that whisper and wail to the rest of the world that we're starting to slip sideways into being fucked up.

They all start out so infuriatingly under the radar. Cloaked in self-sabotage. Designed to go unnoticed, fatally subtle. Mental illness is an abusive, dark shadow. Think Eeyore with unrelenting lightning bolts and fist-sized bullets of hail. And thunder telling you to go fuck yourself.

You need to constantly be on the lookout for all these little, idiosyncratic signs that signal you're starting to lose it.

Anyway, to be a good bipolar, you need to understand your illness, yourself, and take a lot of notes. Here goes it.

For me, depression is listening to an instrumental version of the Pixie's "Where is My Mind?" on repeat. It's feeling fat. It's not eating. It's realizing I'm a failure at everything I do. Realizing that no one truly likes me and I'm full of mistakes—some that already happened and so many more yet to be made. I second guess, I trillionth guess, everything I do. I have no patience for anything, anyone, especially not for myself.

I have no energy for the catastrophe that is me. I start having panic attacks, every day it feels like I'm losing more and more of my right to breathe, my stomach is full of concrete and my eyes won't dry. I can't stop tensing my hands so tightly that my rigid, pained fingers make it practically impossible to crack open my pillbox full of Ativan.

Depression is crying in the car after I hang out with friends because it physically hurts to keep pretending that I am happy. It's fondly remembering how it felt to self-harm, fantasizing over the release I used to get from pooling blood around the point of a pair of scissors, practically drooling over the phantom pain I could cause, getting lightheaded just remembering how such delectable physical pain freed me from emotional wreckage. When I am depressed, I look wistfully at the scars on my body because they remind me of a time when I was free to self-injure, when survival meant dissecting my pain all night long, assuming I had the right number of Band-Aids.

But then again, depression is also dreaming of dying.

Dreaming of letting go and leaving everything and everyone behind. Coming to terms with the fact that you will always be a burden. It's your fault. *Why are you still here?* Stop dreaming already.

For me, hypomania and mania are listening to Grimes too loudly, too often. She's the musician who invented the genre "ADD music;" she's a psychedelic alien sprite, right up my alley.

My desire to hear everything and look at everything and touch everything is insatiable. To others, it looks obsessive, and that's because it is. I want to devour words, noises, colors, laughter. I want to flit around feveriously, and the only thing keeping me paced is the need to rub my hand across brick buildings, smooth countertops, finger fabrics, and caress everything that I deem too tender to pass up.

Strong heightened sensations make me salivate—except I don't need to eat because I'm too beautiful for food.

When I start to cycle, I always get this sly knowing smile that slinks sweetly across my face. It's because I've figured out the universe and I'm the only one in on the secret. But I have a shoddy poker face, so when my husband asks me if I'm "too happy," I can try to lie but he sees how unbelievably sick and happy I am and that I need help.

When my mania revs full force, I rock my body and wring my hands. I'm energized and agitated and I fidget ferociously in a way that is utterly unsatisfying but compulsive. My eyes feel too big for my face, and everything looks louder in both good and bad ways.

"This time, it's different," I always say, "this is the real me."
My speech is pressured, erratic, loud, confusing, and brilliant. I don't recognize myself.

For me, psychosis is being suspicious of my husband's basil plant because it has been looking at me funny all week. I decorate it with office supplies to make it look like a makeshift Christmas tree, like if a mentally unstable Office Depot employee threw an underwhelming, low-budget holiday party. Christening the plant with a purple paperclip "Christmas tree" topper, decorating it with rubberband tinsel, and nesting four grapes at the base to mimic gifts, at first, made the plant less menacing. But ultimately, it never works and I cry to my husband to throw it out, which is a bummer because we both like caprese salads when I'm sane.

When I'm psychotic, I don't trust any food that isn't pre-packaged. My husband knows that things are amiss when I throw out our economy, bulk-size tub of applesauce and insist on buying individual applesauce cups with tight, tamper-proof seals.

The menu of a psychotic leaves little to the imagination.

Hypergraphia hits me hard. If I don't write down exactly what I'm thinking - with 100% correctness - it is the end of the world. I get so mad my hair falls out and I can't see straight. I can probably attribute that to the countless times I've leapt out of the shower, with no time to find my glasses, because I HAD to write down a paragraph that, at the time, was my manifesto, but after the antipsychotics kick in, it is actually just fucking nonsense. Which is devastatingly disappointing. To not be brilliant, after all.

Sometimes I just hug my knees to my forehead and cry on the floor. Or on the bed. Or on the couch. Or in the car, because I'm stuck in skin that's scratchy, loud, vicious, and I'm equal parts dying to be lost forever and frightened of being alone.

Sometimes I hear or see things that aren't there and I wonder if it's the real world or my real craziness - the confusion monopolizes so much of my time. I talk about Princess Diana and Mother Teresa with rave reviews. If these two ladies come up in conversation, my husband knows my meds aren't cutting it. And I'm probably on the verge of cutting myself.

I've lived with this illness for over fifteen years and I've studied myself intently.

I observe my behaviors and analyze my cognitions.

I see a therapist and a psychiatrist,
and a fundamental component of my marriage is talking authentically about my bipolar.

Over the years, I've gotten so much better at comparing my notes with those of my treatment team—at trying to intervene when things start to blur; being proactive to prevent trashing innocent basil plants.

I'm trying so hard to pay attention to the illness and not pretend that the illness is who I am—the "me" that I celebrate and the "me" that I despise.

But with mental illness, it is so hard to be objective.

The illness excels at distracting you and seeping into your skull without you even knowing there was an invasion, so you get sick but it just seems normal. Insanity is status quo. I'm a good bipolar, but it is challenging to successfully track and catch my crazy.

I slip up a lot, it seems. It is exhausting to be hypervigilant 24/7, hoping to catch a glimpse of the beginnings of a brushfire. There's just been a lot on my mind lately because I graduate in May and I need to get a job. I also haven't been sleeping much and I'm pretty fucking tired. Today, I downloaded "Where is My Mind?" by Maxence Cyrin. I totally recommend it. The melancholic nature of the song is so beautiful in the way it lingers and lays heavily across your shoulders. I forgot to pick up my Ativan prescription. I am so completely worthless. It will never get better. *Why am I even here?* I am tired of waking up.

i have half a mind

How do people do it?

Full-time jobs, full-time feelings, full-time relationships, full-time errands, full-time stress, full-time existing? When I try anything full-time, I fall apart. If I work like everyone else, I lose my mind. My full-time bipolar makes me too manic, too psychotic, too depressed, too crazy, and too tired to be useful. I snap in half.

The calendar template for a crazy person leaves plenty of room for doctors' appointments and running to the pharmacy. And ample space for time spent figuring out ways to lie to your boss or your friends or your family so you can convince them that your absence is not sickness but successful busyness. All this punctuated by room in the margins reserved for penciling in low energy, structured activities. Oh, and a few tiny lines for the rest of your life.

I feel overwhelmed just thinking about trying to write my dissertation, publish poems, pretend I'll eventually have a career I can handle, and act like I know how to eat these days. How can other people be so effectively purposeful and efficiently productive? And in complete pieces at the end of the day?

How do people fucking do it?

When I have three meetings in a row, my brain shakes and shudders. Rushing from one appointment to the next makes me break into a cold sweat with a wave of warm queasiness washing over me. Stuck in traffic can end in a panic attack. Staring down at my plate with the expectation of eating can summon a lump in my throat. Getting out of bed, forget it. And all of this collective pathology trickles into my skull, watering my brain with anxiety, agitation, and ache, pooling in the cracked corners of my mind, until the dam breaks and I'm submerged in psychotic depression. Officially on psychiatric house arrest. If

I'm lucky, I have half of my sanity to work with.

How do other people lead their lives?

Full-time lives full of smiles, and cooking homemade dinners, and having babies, and loving partners, and jobs they enjoy and excel at, and healthy bodies that exercise, and beds they sleep in, going to bed at the right time and waking up six hours later, feeling ready to seize the day. Complete with reliable brains that get them everywhere on time. How?

They aren't crazy.

My brain is a disaster - gooey disorder that holds me hostage. This mind of mine threatens to implode every day. The only thing I do full-time is juggle sickness and moments of sane existence one after the other, while, in the meantime, balancing pill bottles, one tablet at a time, to round out the illness I always live in. That's how I do it. A brain steeped in symptoms, wondering how the other half lives.

rapid exhaustion

So much bipolar in the span of several days. Hoping the handful of meds will continue to help and that I can get enough sleep to keep myself settled. It's hard wrestling mania, agitation, fear, depression, hopelessness, energy, brilliant ideas, debilitating loneliness, the need to live fast, and the desire to die all at the same time. Feeling chaotic and crazy. The type of madness that's too hard to hide. Rapid cycling is exhausting. I'm just trying to survive until I cycle through. I wish they would find a cure for this illness.

unless

I am bipolar and it's not a big deal
unless my head cracks open and shatters
and all of the craziness and brilliance
and anger gushes out, followed by howling and laughter.

I am hypomanic and it's not a big deal
unless I try to fuck you or fight,
and I don't eat, I don't sleep, I don't ever come down,
I just dazzle and sparkle every night.

I am manic and it's not a big deal
unless Princess Diana starts cradling my heart
and I cry and I worship, I revere and destroy,
and I don't even mind that I'm falling apart.

I am psychotic and it's not a big deal
unless there's a microphone tucked between my gums
and I weep and I scream, pull my hair and count my teeth,
and wait franticly until Jesus comes.

I am depressed and it's not a big deal
unless I beg and plead with my husband to murder me quickly,
and I lie on the bed, surrounded by pills that don't work,
and take comfort knowing that people will forget me.

I am bipolar and it's not a big deal
until my brain finally backfires and dies
and I'm broken and buried, I'm lost and I'm gone,
only the memory of my madness survives.

this is the *disease* in me

I forgot how much one body could hurt. I forgot how worthless you could feel, even when surrounded by so many people who love you. I forgot how life could be so meaningless, even when you know you have promise.

We all struggle. Life is not easy. Overcoming challenges is a significant part of existing. It just feels hard when there are so many hurdles. But I am a blessed person of privilege. Why do I feel so dark despite all the gifts I've been given? Intellectually, I accept that I am entitled to my feelings, both my joys and my sorrows, but I feel painfully ungrateful. Utterly wasteful. I am invited into so much light. I *should* be happy. On the surface, things look sweet and serene, but right now, on this day and on most likely too many days to come, my smiles are achingly shallow. Why does this disease cut so deeply?

I am poisoned by my illness because, as its potency accelerates, I unwillingly slough off the parts of me that make me proud. This disorder robs me of my identity. I am a positive person. I am a lively spirit. I am an educated advocate. I *should* understand the treacherous nature of this illness. But as soon as I start staggering under the weight of this heavy burden, I am suddenly nothing. This disease turns me into a watered down, blurred version of myself. I am just murky me. More empty than complete. I am just waiting to feel whole. So much time spent waiting.

This is the torment of cycling - always hoping tomorrow will feel better. Trying to treasure every day that you are content and missing this bliss when the sadness sinks in. Stuck in the dim, then in the dark, then in the deepest depression. All you can do is keep hoping again and again.

This is the disease in me.

Anorexia is a parasite that I take out to dinner.

Depression does everything it can to make you feel lonely,
and anxiety does whatever it takes to keep you that way.

my life and suicide

I've been chewing on this for a few weeks - trying to figure out what I want to say and how I want to say it. So far, everything I've written hasn't been able to capture my relationship with suicide. It's not that I don't have something to say, but for a lot of reasons, it's hard to say it. Trying to understand suicide—why someone would take their own life— is frightening and perplexing. Imagine how hard it must be to ask for help.

Suicide makes me think about my middle school boyfriend. Years ago, a mutual friend posted on Facebook that he had taken his own life. They linked his obituary, which was vague, sorrowful, and optimistic. I remember him waiting by my locker before school. I remember sitting together at lunch and holding hands. I remember how we were both struggling with mental illness but didn't know how to talk about it. I hadn't thought about him for well over a decade, but today he sits with me.

A few years ago, I went home to visit my parents and we were chatting about the youth group I attended as a teenager. I mentioned a guy who had been involved with the group and mused out loud, wondering what he was up to. My parents' faces suddenly clouded and they confessed to me that he had died by suicide about eight years prior. I asked them why they didn't tell me and they said they didn't want to upset me. Today, he's on my mind.

I have friends who've attempted suicide and thankfully they are still here today. Some of them talk about their experiences to educate friends and family, others use their story as a way to advocate for change, and others don't share at all but live every single day the best they can. And all of these actions are valued. More importantly, all of these friends are cherished. I think about what life would be like if suicide took over and ended their lives, and it's so hard to imagine a world without them. But, in my own way, I understand. Today in particular, I carry them in my heart.

When Robin Williams died, it felt like losing a father figure. I grew up with the wisdom, warmth, and humor of such characters as Mrs. Doubtfire, the Genie from *Aladdin*, and Batty Koda from one of my favorite films, *Fern Gully*. My parents got me two goldfish when I was a kid, and I named one Robin and the other one Williams. Robin ended up eating Williams, which normally would've been a pretty big blow for a fourth grader, but I knew the real Robin Williams would probably find this funny. Humor gives me hope, and today, Robin Williams is in my smile.

Three attempts. It's hard to remember the details. Honestly, most of it is rather hazy. I do remember the aftermath, and I remember the pain on my parents' and husband's faces much more vividly. To this day, they look at me with love and worry in their eyes and I understand why. But the thing that I wish I could remember the most? Exactly what I was thinking and how it must've felt to be so lost that suicide felt like the only answer. I remember things in snippets: Pouring all of my medication into a cup. The tortured face looking back at me in the mirror. The red on my wrists. The anxiety that I wasn't doing this right and I wouldn't die, failing yet again. The cold night that I walked to the bridge near my house in thin pajamas. When I'm sick, suicide feels like my only answer. It's easy to forget that I'm a fighter. It's easy to forget that I'm a survivor; that the healthy me—the real me—knows how completely loved and worthwhile she is. One of the reasons I am still here is because I am so incredibly blessed to have people in my life who care about me. Who share their hope. Donate perspective. Keep me safe when I'm struggling. It was hard asking for help, there were so many occasions that I just couldn't do it, but my family and friends have always been there for me, no questions asked. With every breath I take - today and every day - I thank my husband and my parents for never giving up on me.

I don't know what else to say, really. I still haven't found the right words. I sit down with my laptop and not much pours out. But lately, I've been significantly more reflective. This past week, I've spent a lot of time thinking about myself, my life, and how happy I am that I'm still here. Sitting with my thoughts, exploring my ideas, digging up the meaning behind my feelings. I'm usually the loudest person in the room, I always have something to say and know how to say it with gusto, but right now, I'm realizing that looking within and trying to understand my illness better—actually, understand myself better—is important for my own recovery. I might never fully understand why I've turned to suicide in the past, but I've come to accept the fact that suicide has always been a part of my life and it may always be, but I am more than my disorder. I deserve a happier ending. Actually, I deserve a life that doesn't focus on endings at all but rather staying present and pushing forward. But there are so many people out there who struggle like I do, and the tragedy is that some of them don't survive. My privilege gave me first, second, and third chances, which, when it comes to mental illness, is a luxury I no longer take for granted. We can't forget the people who've lost their lives to suicide. We have to remember them and tell their stories. We have to challenge the stigma and prejudice that rob people of their existence. We have to challenge ourselves to look within and find our own answers.

For someone who says she doesn't know what to say, I realize I've said quite a bit, but this past week, I've truly been a better listener—to myself and others—than a writer. So while I may not be saying anything right, I'm so fucking grateful that I'm here to at least try and say it.

Thank you so much Mom, Dad, and Spencer.

suicide is static noise

We don't understand mental illness.

I was seventeen when I was introduced to my first psychiatrist and he reassured my parents that he would fix me. My first therapist parroted the same thing. I was fixable. The right treatment and the right amount of compliance would make me better. So I tried to do what I was supposed to, but my bipolar disorder wasn't fixed. I realized that I was the reason I couldn't get better. I broke myself. I was inherently cracked in half. I was worthless.

For years, I lived under the toxic decree that someone with a mental illness can "get better for good," a falsehood that framed experiencing symptoms as the fault of the individual. Believe me, I do what I'm supposed to - psychiatry appointments, meds, therapy, the works - but my mental illness, a chronic illness, will continue to exist as long as I do. It's not my fault that it lurks inside my mind. I'll never be able to evict it. I just need to try to keep it from killing me. I am worthwhile, but I am also sick.

I was inspired to write this after a conversation with a dear friend of mine regarding the existence of another dangerous psychiatric commandment: that suicide is all or nothing. The common belief is that suicide is one-dimensional, a mindset that is mutually exclusive. You either want to kill yourself or you're all better and the thought has completely vanished from your mind. And while that story may feel good to share, as it seemingly inspires hope and it predicts that happy ending we all want, for many people with mental illness, myself included, that isn't our story. Honestly, the fact that this narrative is so frequently regurgitated and imposed on people living with mental illness is harmful. Even fatal. When mentally ill people are told that if we do what we're supposed to do, we won't want to kill ourselves, and then we do all of those things but the urges, cognitions, and feelings around suicide still linger, it is easy to feel like we truly are the broken ones. The worthless. The impossible to save.

But after having this conversation with my friend, the more I think of it, it's true—I can't really be saved. I can't be saved from my illness. My bipolar won't go away. No matter how hard I wish, beg, and plead, it just won't. That's the nature of chronic illnesses. You alleviate the flare-ups and keep moving as best you can. Salvation isn't an option.

I have attempted suicide before. Having suicidal thoughts is a symptom of bipolar disorder. I will always have a relationship with suicide; no one can come in and wipe my mind clean. Suicide is an inescapable part of my life. Every day, on some level, I think about suicide. Suicide is static noise. It is always buzzing in my brain. For **a lot** of people I know who struggle with mental illness, suicide is a constant buzz. But it is a buzz that we suppress, something societal stigma tells us must stay hidden. And framing suicide as an all or nothing experience makes it hard for people to talk about living with an illness that is inextricably linked to suicide. It is a part of our daily struggle and it needs to be talked about. Without a language to discuss **all** aspects of mental illness, more and more people will struggle to ask for help, understand their illnesses, and manage their conditions safely.

I am lucky. For me, suicide is mostly static, something I think about but don't act on. Something I think about but don't often share with others. And while I completely understand that discussing suicide makes the majority of us feel uncomfortable, from my perspective, the fact that I'm talking about my life with suicidal ideation is actually where my hope comes from.

My story doesn't come with a standard "happy ending" in which my suicidal thoughts are suddenly erased, but that doesn't mean I can't have hope. I am hopeful when I can talk about mental illness and people try their best to understand. I am hopeful because I just turned thirty-two years old. My hope is renewed every day that I treat myself kindly.

I don't deserve to be mentally ill. I'm not inherently worthless. I am hopeful. I do the best I can to save myself from the static. I raise my own voice even louder.

hope is often hard to find

One of the most frustrating things about living with a mental illness is that your illness changes over time. You think you've got it all figured out until your brain chemistry pulls sanity out from under you. As you grow up, your illness morphs and mutates, which also means your attitude towards it, your coping mechanisms, and treatment plans have to change, too. That or you're completely fucked. Adapt or let illness take over your life.

The bipolar disorder I had as a teenager looks completely different compared to how it impacts me today. When I was in my late teens and early twenties, my bipolar consisted mostly of hypomanic and manic episodes. Any depression I experienced was pretty mild and it was more of an inconvenience than a troubling aspect of my illness. Let me tell ya, I looooved being hypomanic and manic more than anything in the world. Trust me, if you could dabble in it, you'd be hooked, too. I thought of hypomania and mania as drugs—I mean, that's even how I talk about them today. The language I use is that of an addict struggling to kick their addiction. This was particularly hard considering I could cook up my own customized drug right in my brain whenever I pleased (drugs, risk-taking, not sleeping, and, oh yeah, ditching your meds could do the trick). It's hard to stay sober when that type of high is bubbling at the surface of your brain, waiting for you to just trigger a deluge of euphoria.

But what comes up must come down, so it was inevitable that I'd experience depression. But like I said earlier, when I did slip into a depressive episode, it wasn't that intense. I felt sad and was low energy, but I never felt completely hopeless—thanks, in part, because I knew hypomania and mania were around the corner. I just had to wade through this shallow depression and then I'd be rewarded. All of the terrible things that had happened in my past, the everyday struggles I lived with, all faded when I handed my brain over to my hypomania and mania—no questions asked. Mania was my drug, a vacation from reality, my salvation. It gave me the power to push past negative things in my life and replace them with feelings of grandeur. Back then, I actually thought of my bipolar as a gift. I felt special, magical, superior, like I was the only member of a very elite, exclusive club. Or more accurately, like I built the club and then burned it down and transformed it into a shrine for hypomania and mania. Don't bother lighting a candle because this baby runs on neon lights.

Sometimes I catch myself reminiscing about my life with hypomania and mania. I look back and a small part of me still thinks that life back then was spectacular. It's easy to fall victim to the lies that mental illness whispers to your brain. Mania didn't set me free, it threatened my life. My existence wasn't shiny, beautiful brilliance, it was sickness wrapped in a glittery ribbon. It took me years after I got serious about owning my illness to admit that I used to live a dangerous life. Pushing my brain and body past the brink. I took stupid risks, strained relationships with my irresponsible behavior, and courted disaster when it came to my future. I didn't have the perspective to understand that this was illness. It just felt like identity.

But as I've gotten older, my bipolar disorder has grown darker. Now that I'm in my thirties, my illness is practically unrecognizable. My hypomania and mania are just exaggerated sparkly memories, and instead, I experience mixed episodes—when manic energy and depressed agitation meet. This is often followed by a tidal wave of anger that has no source, which actually drives me even crazier. Really, really, REALLY not fun stuff. And after that angry, futile, anxiety burns off, I plummet into depression. No sliding, no slipping, no sinking, but plummeting like a hopeless rock into a festering depressed cesspool. The depression I live with now is vicious and violent. Under its shadow, all I can think about is giving up. I daydream about getting hit by a bus, succumbing to some mysterious illness that has no cure, of just not waking up. Thinking about suicide becomes part of my everyday routine. It's not that I want to kill myself, it just hurts too much to think about a tomorrow. The depression these days doesn't just linger, it haunts me. The deepest darkest parts typically last for two weeks and then the illness changes again and I find myself feeling muted and subdued, dominated by feelings of dread and anxiety, which soon transform into colorless numbness. I'm no longer suicidal - in part, because I don't have the energy - but I feel hopeless. So incredibly hopeless that I can't even begin to describe it. I feel lost and alone. I feel rubbed raw and utterly broken. I feel estranged from myself. I distance myself from others. Even thinking about that feeling sends shivers down my spine and oozes cement into my stomach. It is a feeling that robs me of myself. It's terrifying.

The thing is, naturally, I'm a happy person, and thus, my personality syncs well with my hypomanic-manic self. And hypomanic-manic-me as well as the real me are a serious departure from my depressed self. A huge part of my self-care is telling myself that depression isn't the real me and surrounding myself with people who remind me that I am more than this black void. And I also have to remind myself that hypomanic-manic-me isn't the real me either. Whatever the illness tells me, I have to confront it and provide a better answer. But when I'm sick, that feels like an overwhelming, ominous, nearly impossible task.

One of my deepest fears is that - despite everything I've done to manage my bipolar - one of these depressive episodes will break my brain. Change me forever. I won't just lose hypomania and mania, baggage from my past that I try not to care about, but I'll stop being happy. I'll stop being myself. Depression will pummel me into a miserable person. I'm frightened that I am going to be erased and drawn back as nothing but an embodiment of disease. I'm putting the work in, I'm adapting, I'm trying my best, but, at times, I feel defeated. What I once saw as a gift, I now know is a curse. My illness is changing and I can't help but wonder if I'll have enough of the real me left to keep me moving forward with life on my terms. I just can't give up.

When we talk about mental health, it's easy to get distracted by the allure of quick fixes and saccharine mantras. For example, touting yoga as a cure-all and sharing feel good messages on Instagram - *Just love yourself!* - typed in flowy font set against a sunrise. And I think the most damning thing of all is the fact that we see significantly more white people having these conversations compared to people of color. None of this is easy. Hope is often hard to find. And while I know that having diverse narratives about mental health is integral to fighting stigma, I think we also have to talk about *mental illness.* The fact that mental illnesses leave us messy and exhausted and shaky on our feet. That they challenge our sense of self-worth and our sense of self. That they make neurotypical people uncomfortable, which can actually be productive when it comes to redefining mental health and mental illness. But here's the thing, if we make living with mental illness seem easy, we're inadvertently telling people that if they struggle then it's their fault. Not all stories have happy endings, but we should still talk about them with the energy and amplification that we reserve for tidier interpretations of mental health. Because that's reality. That's representation. Today, I can't end on a high note, I don't have it in me, but I'm here, and I'm typing, and I'm doing my best. And I know I'll have more to say when I'm ready. Thanks for listening.

habit

People are nothing but their patterns. Slaves to foreseen cycling. Chasing habit after habit.
It is hard to imagine changing when we only see a future that feels just like today.

when things fade

I just realized I've forgotten the sound of my grandpa's voice.

the emaciation of depression: the story of my collapsing ashes

My heart and head dip and sag from loneliness. My insides are so empty and emaciated that my body is wrinkling, curling, crinkling inwards to try and fill it with something, even something so crumbled at the corners. I am a clump of old tired leaves that are decomposing into crestfallen crisped edges, tucked clumsily inside my skin.

My heart continues to starve as more and more dust clogs its gasping cavities. This brittle implosion is really just a meager, decaying attempt to make me a bit more whole. Cannibalizing my own gristle and bone, desperately seeking some kind of stuffing, to keep my ever-collapsing shape even the slightest bit upright.

All my little sad thoughts are piled high, making an immense pyramid of nothing. I feel hollow, but my head is heavy. I lack worth, value, meaning. My head throbs with dismal deprivation. I ache from the core of my dusty heart. Each sob swirls my valves' debris like a snow globe built with blood. When I am this sad, I feel it in my body, I see it all around me, I taste bitterness in my mouth, and nothing sounds like it should.

Because I feel alone. Completely alone.

Left with useless mortal dust and entombed in poignant loss.

I feel so utterly alone, and that hopelessness is just stuck to me. Stuck inside me. Fucking stuck. I can't shake it. I can't escape it. I wrestle with a body that I hate so deeply, a body that is now too weak to stumble. I clutch my cracked heart and feel the sadness spin inside my chest, disintegrating specks swirling tightly, coalescing into the nodule jammed inside my throat, and shedding suffocating dust that settles in my asphyxiating stomach. My mealy heart erupts, spraying flares of fleshy soot that signal my body is caving in, giving up, and surrendering to a fate of defeated particles of charcoal. I am so alone in this agony.

Alone, but still alive.

big fat blessing

I have always hated my stomach. It was fat and flabby. It was disgusting and un-lovable. No matter how hard I dieted, how vicious my anorexia was, my belly was always betraying me. My stomach was responsible for all of my unhappiness. My stomach was the reason I'd always be alone. No matter how hard I tried to live solely on air and agony, I still had to eat (because, you know, I'm a person), but eating felt like failing. Which meant my stomach was a sign of weakness. A big, fat, gross sign of weakness. I didn't just have unreal expectations - craving a thin, perfect, beautiful, beloved body - I was utterly hopeless and addicted to the idea that my worth was quantified by my weight. It wasn't just a struggle to be happy. Over the years, I battled suicidal thoughts and self-harmed because I felt like I didn't belong and I didn't think I deserved to exist. I was cursed.

I remember one time in elementary school, a kid pinched the "flubber" on my stomach. I remember my grandma squeezing my fat rolls because I was "this close" to being beautiful. I remember how the very thought of taking off my shirt gave me panic attacks. I was taught that my humiliating belly was meant to stay hidden. But I'm about to turn thirty-three, and I've come a long way.

I don't fixate on the size of my jeans. I don't own a scale. I don't hate myself when I eat a cookie (or multiple cookies!). I define beauty for myself. No matter what I weigh, I am enough, I am worthwhile. I'm beautiful and, more importantly, I am brave. I've learned to not just make peace with the part of me that I blamed for my misery for so long, but to truly love my soft, curvy belly. It's taken a lot of hard work and I'm proud to say that my relationship with my body has gotten better and better over the past few years (thanks therapy!). But, of course, some days are better than others.

Yesterday was a bad body image day. I was walking my dogs and listening to music when "Water Me" by Lizzo popped up next on my playlist. As I glanced at my phone, I saw her album cover blanket my screen. I stared in awe. She was the most sensual, confident, desirable, and empowered woman I'd ever seen. There she was, with a body that looked like mine, a body that deserved space and demanded to be seen without embarrassment or shame. I took a screenshot and stashed it in my favorites folder so I'd have a reminder that bodies like mine have the right to exist. To take up space. To be proud of. To love and be loved.

Big bellies are the final frontier of represented beauty. We've embraced big breasts, butts, and thighs. But I've decided that I'm not going to wait for bodies like mine to be celebrated and included in fashion ideals. I'm going to appreciate my big belly and my large body because, well, why shouldn't I? Life is about being happy, not about fitting in. I'm taking back my body and my power. Like Lizzo, like Lindy West, like Jessamyn Stanley, like Jes Baker. Whether or not you like it, we're not going anywhere.

So I want to say thanks to all of the fat women (both cis and trans) who push back on the narrow standards of what it means to be a woman with their strong, lovely fat bodies. Let's never be silenced or erased. Let's make it safer for us to live as our true selves in whatever shape we take. To all of my soft, curvy, heavy, fat, large - whatever language you want to use - friends, we don't have to apologize or hide, because our bodies are blessings.

Big ones.

aggressive deprivation

Depression is aggressive deprivation. It steals the love from your heart and the light from your eyes. You lose yourself to nothingness. It robs you of your joy, of sincere smiles, of laughing out loud. Depression takes away your friends, your will to live, it hurts your family, and it tells you that you will always be broken.

But depression also buries you. Destroys you by lacing throbbing aches through your too-tight joints, by force-feeding you a congealed lump of disappointment, bile, and self-disgust that clogs your stomach, by lodging a stabbing headache behind red-rimmed eyes that haven't slept nearly enough. Depression rips taste from your tongue and rubs your skin raw, leaving it tender to the touch. Even hugs hurt so much that your body shakes and threatens to cave in as someone moves lovingly around you.

Depression makes me forget who I am. It steals me from myself. It tells me I will feel like this forever. Depression is an illness that does everything in its power to deprive you of a life worth living. Depression does its best to drown you in inconsolable disease. It is a dangerously persuasive sickness. But no matter how long it empties words from my mouth, smothers my spark, and tells me everything would be better if I just stopped existing, I'd like to believe I will always, always have enough hope to keep going.

a life with spiders

I am nothing but a broken body that is too tired to keep on clinging.

Too exhausted to put her head on straight.

I slip into a dark sadness that is penetrated by muffled words spoken in hushed therapist tones. I hear concerned sighs followed by words like "dissociation" and "catatonic."

I hear my husband whisper love letters into my throbbing temples. I feel the weight of his hand rub the small of my back, directly on my skin, just how I like it.

But I am imprisoned in this ripped, ragged, and raw skin-skeleton castle of a body that weeps too loudly and burns too softly.

I detest this sagging skin. My flanks of fat are disgusting. I am embarrassed that I ever lived a life in this baggy body, just begging to be set ablaze.

Everything about me is on fire, aching and slow. Hopelessness inflates my sputtering lungs with puffs of stifling fevered air that eventually shred my chest like collapsing hot air balloons.

Tears stream out of boiled red eyes and they slash scars into my face with their hot steam. I can almost smell my cheeks burning. My chapped lips taste like salt and blood. My nose runs into the corners of my mouth. I can't seem to wipe any of it away.

The fire licks my spine and I cannot walk, let alone stand up.

Nothing is working.

Why am I still like this?

I beg my husband to kill me - to wrap his strong hands around my scalding neck and snuff out the fire smoldering in my chest. Extinguish the poison embers rattling around my skull. To turn out the lights in my eyes.

To die would be a relief. Blissful release.

To stop existing would mean everything to me.

He says no. He loves me, but he says no.

For the very first time, I see things that aren't there - spiders with stick figure legs. I am too tired to be frightened, except for that first morning when black legs raced across my ceiling and I catapulted out of bed, suddenly full of energy because it was either them or me.

My psychiatrist says that hallucinations happen, and if I can remind myself that round black dots encircled with eight black pointed lines are not real then I'll be alright.

I give up on my life with skittering spiders above me - a life that moors me to my bed.

My parents come to help take care of me, and my dad and I bake banana bread with chocolate chips. My mom buys me red lipstick.

By the time they leave, I can walk the dogs on my own and I don't fall asleep praying that I won't wake up.

I still wake up to flashes of seething spiders overhead, but I think I'll be alright.

My husband can finally touch my skin without pulling back scalded strong fingers.

My depression has gotten so much worse.

Is this how it will always be?

memories from when
i didn't eat

My stomach acid carved angry weeping holes throughout my body, so I dreamt of nothing but my own internal curio cabinet of decay, stocked with countless cupboards full of corporal gristle and calcified hopelessness.

Evidence of my emptiness and fat failure on display.

Secret treasures I wanted to save and see at the same time,
bragging with my new thin body while desperately hiding my drastic measures.

Scarred esophagus, scoured enamel. Blurred vision, unshakable risk of fainting.

First hunger, then pain, and lasting defeat; things that tortured me at night.

My blood seeped through this heap of morbid oddities, past my trophy case of disordered eating, as sopping shards of life leached out and I continued to die with a smile.

I was the thinnest I had ever been, but instead of enjoying it, I was selfishly dying.

I've struggled with disordered eating my entire life. For so many years, my relationship with my body was incredibly toxic. It hurt me and I would hurt it.

Anorexia, bulimia, over-eating, orthorexia - these were the clinical words used to describe and diagnose how I treated myself. But the shared root motivating these destructive behaviors and my disastrous attitude was the fact that I felt completely worthless, out of control, and unsafe.

My body made me vulnerable and I deeply resented it.

I acted on this internal pain through harmful external actions - starving, cutting, burning, vomiting, and eating until I was sick. I'm not 100% comfortable in my own skin, but I love myself more than I ever have before. I love everything that makes me who I am: my experiences, my humor, my intelligence, my resilience, and the body that I'm finally learning to love.

This is a strong body.

A body whose vulnerability makes her beautiful.

suicide sounds so soft. death seems like such a gentle landing. embrace this peace and let the ending begin. comfort in kind killing.

please.

see brightness

"Do my eyes still sparkle?" she asks,

knowing full well they don't shine as they darken and dim.

Depression sneers in her face with a snap and a bite,

"Your eyes are nothing but empty, and that's how they've always been."

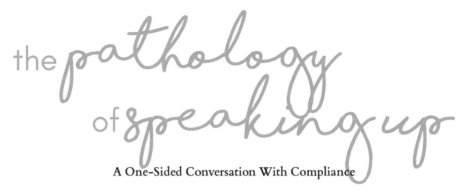

the pathology of speaking up

A One-Sided Conversation With Compliance

Hi, yes, I'd like to file a complaint. Oh, against Geodon. That name isn't on file? Um, let me think.

Sorry it's taking me awhile to think of it. Funny, that's one of the reasons I'm filing this complaint. Ziprasidone! That's it!

Wait, what did you say—oh, why am I on it? I have bipolar I disorder. Yeah, I have what it says on the bottle: "acute manic or mixed episodes."

Oh no, I have both acute manic *and* mixed episodes. Yeah, um, it is pretty rough. You need to know the type of medication it is? The bottle says it is a "pyschotropic medi-cation" and an "atypical antipsychotic." I wouldn't say it sounds "scary," I mean, this is my life. This is my diagnosis.

Oh sorry, you need to know why I'm filing this complaint, right. I guess, I'll start with this: my thinking is a lot slower now that I'm on it. Significantly slower. I'm tired all the time, too. No, seriously, my thinking is really fucking sluggish - it makes me anxious. No, I wasn't always "slow like this." Sorry, I'll calm down.

I also have these slight tremors, they kind of freak me out. I feel like I don't have any control over my body, honestly. Um, yeah, I understand that the meds are supposed to help me, but Geodon is making it worse.

I'm not symptomatic, you're right, but I'm not myself either. That is why I'm filing this complaint. I want my brain back. I know it's broken, yes, that's why I'm sick in the first place, but I want to try other medications.

What? Yes, I tried to discuss this with my psychiatrist. He didn't, um - he didn't listen. He doesn't have time. He has a lot of patients. I-I know I'm lucky I have access to a doctor, yeah, I'm not saying—I'm not trying to be ungrateful. I-yeah, I'll wait, you can put me on hold.

Hi, no, no, I'm here! I'm here. Someone put me on hold. Can I file my complaint now, please? The Geodon is making me feel worse, it isn't helping. Yeah, I'm not "sick," but I'm not any better. I'm too sedated. My brain feels so heavy, it's hard to think.

Um, yeah, I understand I'm lucky that I have a psychiatrist *and* insurance *and* enough money to cover my co-pays. Yeah I-I understand that. I've heard this before - I hear this a lot actually. Look, I'm trying to go off Geodon because *it isn't working!* The side effects are just as bad as my symptoms, worse even! I'll go on something else. Please. Anything else!

No, no, no, no, not Depakote. That doesn't work for me - there should be a note about it in my file. I've been on it before and it *really* fucks me up. Sorry, I'll calm down.

Wait, you're transferring me to my psychiatrist? No, he doesn't get it. I told you, he doesn't listen! I want to file a complaint! That's why I called.

Geodon isn't working and I need to start over - try something new. I can't live with this stuffy, clogged up brain. It's like my thoughts are trudging through quicksand.

No, no, I told you, I don't want to talk to my psychiatrist. He's a part of the problem, too, actually. He doesn't listen to me, he just prescribes me pill after pill and tells me to wait—wait to see what works. Sit and wait. How long do I have to wait? Put my world on pause? Like I don't have a life outside this diagnosis. And I-I tell him it's not working, and he says that I "seem less emotional." But that's just because Geodon feels like a fucking tranquilizer. I'm numb, I'm nothing. I'm dizzy, I'm empty. There's not even a tiny spark of light glimmering inside me anymore. I can't feel anything at all. Do you understand? This medication makes me unrecognizable.

No, no, I'm not trying to cause trouble. I'm compliant, I swear. I thought this was a complaint line? No, I'm not taking myself off my meds. I-I- yes, I'm thankful I have access to this care. I really am, I just, I don't want to be sick, but I don't want to suffocate under all these pills either. I don't feel crazy, but I don't feel anything at all.

Wait, what? Please don't put me in the hospital! I'll deal with it on my own, okay?

I'll take my meds, I won't complain. I'll withdraw my complaint, everything will go back to normal, I promise!

I'll wait, I'll be patient, I'll be the best patient, I'll listen to my psychiatrist, yeah, you're right, he knows what he is doing. He is the doctor, after all. I'll let him make the decisions, okay? I'll behave. I'll be better. I'll be quiet. Just don't put me in the hospital. I'll do what you think is best. You know what is best for me.

I'm crazy, after all, you're right. *I'm the crazy one.* What was I thinking?

Thank you, I'm so sorry I bothered you.

Have a nice day.

this head of mine

I can't keep up with this head of mine

that stockpiles sorrow in the back of my skull,
that roasts my eyes until they're charred, black, and dull,

a rotting, festering brain like this
that sinks my consciousness into nausea and nothingness.

I can't keep up with this head of mine

that resigns my ears to vengeful hissing, spitting, and ringing,
that poisons, panics my lungs, each breath wet and stinging,

A rotting, festering brain like this
that furrows my body with acidic erosion, a sinewy apocalypse.

I can't keep up with this head of mine

that blankets rank sludge and wet rubbish wall-to-wall in my gut,
that laces grit and grime through my mouth, wiring my bloody gums shut,

a rotting, festering brain like this
that pollutes, electrocutes, and carves angry grins into my wrists.

I can't keep up with this head of mine

that pummels my heart into a mish-mash of innards and debris,
that grips and rips my shoulders until it shakes my soul free,

a rotting, festering brain like this
isn't worth saving, or loving - just flood this fucking cranial abyss.

I can't keep up with this head of mine

that's broken and gnarled and sick all the time,

and I can't help but wonder if it's really bipolar that's rotting my brain
or if I'm just a terrible, burdensome being that's actually quite sane.

I want to turn off my thoughts and cry until there's nothing left to say,
and lie down in the sewer and watch myself ruthlessly decay.

I can't keep up with this.

she's right

I remember how she grew furiously exasperated
as I winced and wriggled and aspirated.
My lungs clogged with snot and tears and feeble gasping,
and I tried to croak out, my voice strained and rasping,
to beg for forgiveness, to plead, pant, and cry,
to barter with her as I started to die.
She stood on my throat and she spat in my ear,
telling me soon all my family and friends would be here,
and they'd all laugh in my face and dig into my wrists,
and whisper through sneers that I'd never be missed.
I cried and I struggled to get off the ground.
I blinked as the heel of her boot came crashing down,
and with a skull-fracturing crunch, she scrambled my brain,
and she stifled my screams until I drooled from the pain.
Then I bit off my lips and I clawed off my skin,
I could no longer tell where I ended and she started, how did this begin?
Either way, I look in the mirror and all I see is fatness and disgust,
and despite what anyone says, she's the only opinion I trust.
It's not that I'm bipolar or mentally ill, it's not a disease.
She's right, I'm broken and worthless, you're better off without me.

Sometimes my sadness is soft.
Soft and familiar.

I can curl up against it, sink into it, surrendering to the quiet, familiar aching.
I know this pain and, in a way, it's comforting to dissolve into a sorrow that asks nothing of me.

To relax and readjust to feeling hopeless again, but at least less nervous.

My heart stops racing as my head bows, my thoughts stop whirring as my energy slows, and, in a way, my depression is a break from agitated anxiety and frenetic irritability.

Sometimes it feels easier to be sad and disassemble all expectations.
People ask nothing of me when I lie in bed all day, inviting depression to tuck me under the covers.

I find solace hiding in my sadness when the world is exhausting and giving up feels like a much-needed vacation.

My depression is a "do not disturb" sign that I smear across my face, as my body crumples from too much softness and not enough structure, as I sacrifice my everyday life and all ambition just so I can mimic not existing.

Soft and suffocating.
Sometimes my sadness takes over my life, and I let it.

unbearable

Depression is not about wanting to die.
Depression is about wishing you never existed.

Depression poisons your logic. And while its perspective is initially unfamiliar, it speaks to you so fluently that it soon makes sense. It tells you how much you hurt others around you. How you make them worry, how you inconvenience them, how you make them feel unsettled, and how you hold them back. They are the truest words you've ever heard and you agree that you're nothing but a burden. And here's the thing – the reality is that the last thing you want to do is kill yourself and put anyone through more pain, but you can barely handle the hurt much longer. And it feels like you don't have many options.

Your existence has always been so exhausting.

Depression is marked not by the back and forth counterarguments between killing yourself and trying to live, but by the deafening desire to cease existing. A feat that is completely and frustratingly unattainable. Living hurts, chasing after death hurts others, and the only thing you want is impossible to reach because no matter what, someone is harmed. You can't flick a switch and un-exist. Go back in time and erase yourself from everybody's life. If you could, Lord knows you would.

Depression is a holding cell.
Depression is the liminal space in which you are stuck between life and death.

Depression is the triangulation between irresponsible death, hopeless life, and the unfettered but unfeasible dream to have never been born.

I am so stuck and so lost.

my depression

My depression is going to a job I love and sobbing the entire car ride home.

My depression is having my husband prop me up in the shower because I'm so empty, it's hard to stand.

My depression is canceling dinner plans with a dear friend because eating is just too hard.

My depression is years of practice learning how to disguise numbness with a passable smile.

My depression is sleeping on top of my laundry because, at the end of the day, I have no energy left to fold anything.

My depression is crying into my dog's fur because I love her so much, but my body aches so badly I can't take her on a walk.

My depression is feeling lonely, even when everybody tells me how much they love me.

My depression is hopelessness that luckily will not last forever.

I will be okay. I always am.

When mental illness is just a part of your life.

alone

Every time he tells me, "You are my world,"
I am saddened that his heart lives on such a shattered planet.

on our terms

It hurts to feel the world gasp. She prays for mercy from everyday murder,
I hear her begging. My heart seizes with every tortured sigh.

She calls out to simply turn off her stars.

She pleads for a quicker and finite death because she can't continue watching us.
We bring her slow decay and deliberate destruction.
Her unflinching children intent on making her suffering last.

There is nothing for her to do but keep time with her wounds
and wait for the day we push her to perish.

We light her goodbyes on fire.

the end

The Catholic church three blocks behind my house is setting off fireworks. Flashes and bangs, fizzing and popping, and incessant sparkling and snapping are taking over the neighborhood. The night sky is alive and angry with a melee of overlapping, mismatching, clashing, tacky, neon lights. This Sunday marks the end of the bazaar.

Growing up, a Jew from out of town, I was completely unaware of the Catholic Church's love affair with 50/50 raffles, fried dough, and Chinese auctions. Only after moving to Pittsburgh, I learned that the annual bazaar is where you eat fried Oreos in the name of Christ and gamble in praise of the Lord.

My dad, a Jew from out of town, remarks that he's surprised the city allows this tiny neighborhood church to set off such considerable fireworks, considering there are trees everywhere. We stand side by side on the deck. We slowly shift back and forth, from right to left, in sync, clearly an inherited behavior. I pause our marching so I can rest my head on his shoulder. My parents are heading back home tomorrow morning and I already miss them.

In between the dazzling lights and explosive pulsing, you can see the echoes of the fireworks, my favorite part. Echoes are the blurred grey shadows only visible when one firework flares out, right before another erupts. These echoes form daunting figures in the night sky; taking the shape of an enormous ghostly rib cage, of charcoal tentacles etched in the blackness above my house, a colorless collection of long spidery legs unfurling and taking over every angle of the sky.

I like these phantom murky afterthoughts, these inky shapes absent of color. I like reconfiguring their outlines in my mind so I see nothing but the leftover bones of dusty skeletons, catching them before the smog bleeds out into the emptiness of the atmosphere.

I've always preferred these cloudy echoes to the scratchy gold, purple, pink, and green pipe cleaner shaped fireworks thrown predictably, uncreatively, and haphazardly into the night sky. I take a deep breath, sizing up my small backyard and the patch of sky above my house, where every other night, the only things we see are the silhouettes of trees, power lines, and occasionally bats, which I intentionally refer to as "birds" to make me feel less creeped out. It's surprising how well that works.

My mother, husband, and two dogs stay inside. My husband doesn't give a shit about fireworks and my dogs are hiding beneath his chair and between his legs, but I hear my mom say something like, "Impressive for such a tiny church!"

Soon enough, their sounds start to sizzle softer and softer, and their bright colors fade to dishwater black and grey, and soon enough there's not enough light to see the smoke-fueled creature that's wrapped its echoing talons possessively around my neighborhood.

My husband looks up from his book, "They do this every year."

But I know that it's the end of the world.

better days

Finding balance is the hardest thing ever. No, actually *staying* balanced is the hardest thing ever. Because staying balanced requires constant maintenance and a dedicated sense of self-awareness. Keeping yourself steady takes work and you're never done, you're always working - always trying to get there and stay there. And part of the pursuit is accepting the fact that you'll inevitably falter and fail but you can't give up, you just have to keep going. We all have good, bad, and better days.

I get it, I know that no one is truly balanced - we all buoy back and forth between extremes – but I think it's harder for people living with bipolar disorder. With our moods fluid and our feelings almost always in flux, we often live in the extremes. Mania on one end, depression on the other. Life with an illness made of contradicting arguments. A tricky tug-o-war. For us, staying healthy requires a highly vigilant routine of self-reflection, reality checks, actually listening to others' observations and hearing their concerns, and following through on individualized interventions when we start slipping. Slipping and stumbling is certain, but the "when," "where," and "how" aren't predictable.

But here's the thing, our quest for balance is made all the more difficult because our brains crave chaos. We're working with a disease whose archenemy is balance. Existing with an illness that tells us to unravel. We chase our mania and then fall apart during our depressions. A constant to and fro. From one vicious pole to the other. We may want to live in the middle of this ill continuum but it's challenging to stay alert, in charge, and capable when facing such a treacherous, seductive disease. Balance is a battlefield.

Bipolar is a disorder that mimics identity. Convincing you that being manic is just being the best version of yourself. Telling you that you deserve your mania – you are extraordinary and deserve to be extraordinarily happy. Not just happy, ECSTATIC. You slog through the depressions, fighting the hopelessness and worthlessness, pushing through the pain and the lethargy, and mania is your reward! For many people living with bipolar, it can take years to admit that you need help, finally saying goodbye to denial and manic lust, and coming to terms with the reality that you are sick. But it's not who you are and you can get better. What you really deserve is being healthy *and* happy. But after this difficult declaration, things don't necessarily get easier. The irony of treating bipolar disorder – doing what it takes so you can pursue a sane, more balanced, truer version of yourself - is that the very tools you're given to keep your illness in check can push you over the edge of sanity, in either direction - sometimes, in seemingly subtle ways, starting out well-intentioned and then escalating into disaster.

Let me explain. If I don't sleep enough, I run the risk of becoming manic. If I sleep too much, it can awaken my depression. If I take an antidepressant to help me during particularly nasty depressive episodes, I have to be careful because too much of that type of medication can trigger my mania. My happy lamp that I use to combat Pittsburgh's grey winters works wonders, but too many minutes in front of this lil' light bulb can lure my mania out of hibernation. The medication I take that keeps me together, that allows my brain to mimic a sense of normalcy, that provides me stability I can't produce on my own, is therapeutic until I take too much and overdose. At my fingertips is too much or too little. Too fast or too slow. Too strong or too weak. Too far or not far enough. Balance is always in jeopardy. My brain and body are in the crossfire. I'm constantly seeking the in-between and trying not to lose hope when it gets harder and harder. I have to remind myself that I'm in charge, not my illness. We all have good, bad, and better days.

Balance is a bitch. Balance with bipolar is a monster. Staying healthy is an every day labor of love - loving yourself especially on the days you don't feel worth it. I'm trying really hard to put the real me first, to stay safe, and remind myself that illness isn't identity. I'm in control and I deserve to live my own life, not be a host to parasitic mental illness. I'm a work in progress and that's okay. We all are, crazy and sane alike. But it's hard when I start veering one way or another and I need to adjust, re-orient, get my balance back, especially when I'm already too far gone. I have to remind myself that I'm not a failure, this isn't my fault, this is mental illness. It's constant. It camouflages. It can be hard to understand. It never ends. It can be so fucking exhausting. Some days, it feels like too much. I'm my own version of Sisyphus, a new spin on an old favorite, as I trudge along, rolling my prescription bottle of antipsychotics, bearing down and shoving my way up Pittsburgh's hills. I make it to the top, and then watch as the lid pops off and my pills scatter down the hillside. Then I proceed to collect them and I start all over again, heading to the hilltop, day after day. Settling into the reality of living mentally ill. Accepting and understanding that there are two sides of every mood disorder, stability and cycling, in my case, mania and depression, and the true me who exists somewhere in between. A lifetime of looking beyond illness to find myself. To find my balance. To find my peace.

my illness my voice my life

"Recovery."

I know it's a popular term in the mental health community, but I've never really liked using the word "recovery" to describe grappling with my own mental illness. And while it may seem like a minor thing to puzzle over, when it comes to dismantling stigma, it is important to remember that words matter- particularly when finding language that empowers you to understand and explain your illness. Even after all these years, I'm still figuring things out, but I wouldn't call it "recovery." I guess maybe it's because I'm not so much focused on the recovery of something lost, instead I'm doing what I need to do to keep on existing.

I started experiencing the early tickling of bipolar disorder when I was fifteen and I was formally diagnosed at seventeen. Like a lot of bipolars, I come with a history of PTSD and have juggled my fair share of addictions, namely anorexia and an affinity for drugs. Throughout high school and college, I was a messy, un-medicated, self-destructive, and, at times, delightfully chaotic puzzle piece of a person. I was so enamored with mania and dedicated to believing it was the true me that I entertained a handful of unhealthy behaviors because they helped keep me in the throes of my preferred shade of madness.

I didn't know how to be a person. I just knew how to be a bipolar person. How to induce mania with speed, Adderall, cocaine, and ecstasy, how to keep myself buzzing viciously bright by not sleeping for days, how to maintain my high by not eating and embracing hypersexuality, and how to self-injure - carving secret wounds undetectable to most eyes - when I needed a shock of pain to kick my capacity for heightened sensations up a notch. I knew how to refill my prescriptions at the pharmacy like clockwork and pick them up religiously so it appeared that I took them even though I squirreled them away in the crevices and corners of my bedroom. I knew how to go to my therapy appointments and expertly pantomime the charade of plausible sanity and successfully not raise any suspicions.

I had it all figured out. I didn't need any help.

Except when I inevitably crashed and I was swept away in vicious swells of psychotic depression. That's when I fell apart, because my architectured manic reality was perpetually unsteady and predictably prone to collapse. It was only a matter of time.

I wasn't always aware of it, but I lived a life where capsizing was always just a matter of time. My episodes had expiration dates. But after a lot of triggers, turmoil, and close calls, I finally grew up. I realized that at the rate I was going I would also have an expiration date. Prioritizing this illness over real life, and the people who truly mattered to me, was not only reckless and irresponsible but life threatening. I grew tired of almost dying. Of trying to die.

Bipolar disorder is exhausting, especially when you don't treat it. After college, I made the decision with conviction that I wanted to live. I was finally going to take a long look at my illness, learn to understand it, and stop making excuses. I promised to take care of myself. And I learned that I couldn't do it alone. I found support groups and mentors but, more importantly, I found my own voice. I figured out that existing meant asking for help.

During those early days of piecing together my life and sifting through the echoes of illness to unearth my identity, I was introduced to the term "recovery." The idea of recovering from mental illness. Reclaiming your sanity, your health, regaining possession of your life. While I appreciate the term and I am glad it works for many other people in my community, it has never proven to be an accurate description for my own experience with mental illness. I never felt that "recovery" was the right word, the right lens even, to frame my life with bipolar. But I didn't have anything else.

I was chatting with a friend this morning, a woman who fondly refers to herself as a "professional crazy person," and we both shared stories of other people, mostly neurotypical individuals, correcting us on our self-definitions.

"Oh no! You aren't bipolar, you *have* bipolar disorder."

And while the intent is usually good, there is nothing more irritating than someone telling you what words to use. What language you should use. Especially when it's about how you should think and talk about yourself. My friend and I clinked our cups and talked about what illness means to us on a personal level. What we think about our disorders and how we talk about them. How we anchor our identities in a world where mental illness is sorely misunderstood and those who live with it are often silenced. I left the coffee shop with a lot on my mind.

I have lived with bipolar for a long time and I have a relationship with my illness - finally, a healthy one. And cultivating your own language, finding your own voice to talk about your illness, is empowering. It's a critical step in taking care of yourself. After this morning's slice of cake and chai latte, I started seriously thinking about the words I use to tell my own story, both to myself and others. I asked myself why I kept recycling the word "recovery" when it didn't authentically reflect my experience. I finally realized that, for me, it's not about "recovering." It is about existing. It is about learning how to be a person who navigates the world every day and narrates her own story in her own words. I have built a safe and loving support network, I have collected the right resources and tools, I know how to ask for help when I need it, and all this enables my existence. I'm no longer a bipolar person. I'm in charge.

I don't think of myself as recovering - returning to a plane of sanity that I never truly had. I don't think of myself as re-discovering past moments of stability and health. Truthfully, I don't think I've ever had a healthy baseline. But I've learned to move forward. I set my sights on finding new peace, on making better decisions. I celebrate every day and plan for the next one. I'm getting so much better at managing my life.

For me, it's not about recovery. It's about championing my own existence. Working hard to keep on existing. Carving out a life on my own terms. Doing whatever it takes. Those are my words and this is my life.

I choose to exist.

FIVE

existing

i don't thank my *bipolar* for a single thing

and I love reading all of the narratives that are swirling about social media. There are so many different voices, different identities, and different experiences that are amplified, and every single one of these perspectives matter. When there are more storytellers, there is less stigma. For someone living with a mental illness, it is heartening to read and watch these accounts of what life is like living, struggling, and succeeding with a mental illness, and how this isn't a linear adventure. These stories are familiar and I see aspects of my own experiences embedded in so many of these journeys, but I still need to tell my own story, using my own words.

> Hi, I'm Rachel.
> I don't thank my bipolar.
> For anything.
> Not a single thing.

Many mental health narratives hash out how illness can make one stronger, how, in a way, illness is a gift because it can increase one's capacity for compassion, or how mental illness has provided a profound sense of purpose when it comes to educational and professional goals. How illness makes us better. I think these perspectives are incredibly important, but nuh-uh, that ain't me.

This is me: Living with bipolar disorder is the worst! As I've learned how to best manage my mental illness and practice self-care, life has gotten much more predictable and a bunch easier, but things are undoubtedly harder living with a partially busted brain. I'm lucky that medication and therapy work really well for me, but even then, bipolar disorder blows major chunks. This isn't about pity mongering. This is about the truth that bipolar disorder sucks serious nards. That's my anthem - this illness fucking sucks, but I don't.

If I could take a pill that would cure me, I would snatch it right out of your hand and swallow it dry. Because my bipolar disorder doesn't make me special, it makes my life complicated. My bipolar disorder doesn't make me brave. It's not the source of my strength. It lingers under the surface of my consciousness, wheedling into my brain and poisoning how I feel about myself and how I experience the world. I'm special, brave, strong, and talented without my illness. Bipolar disorder isn't a trial that I need to tackle in order to show the world I'm tough enough. I don't need an illness to exaggerate my awesomeness. With an illness that mimics identity, it can be hard to tell where bipolar ends and I begin—the boundaries are never that distinct—but my bipolar disorder isn't a badge. It's a label, a diagnosis, a hefty, troublesome detail. My bipolar doesn't get to take a bow.

As I mentioned, many mental health narratives tip their hat to illness, considering disorder to be a catalyst for strength, which brings us to the question of the hour: has my bipolar disorder made me stronger? Do I wear it at a jaunty angle? Well, yes, because pushing through adversity always makes someone stronger. Surviving and thriving under the weight of adversity encourages and expands upon one's capacity for resilience. It can make you see life in a new light. But I'd like to think that I would be a compassionate and well-rounded human being even if I didn't have a mental illness. Mental illness isn't my identity, it's not a shiny accessory, it's something I have that I hate. It's my kryptonite, it's not a superpower. I'd give it away in a hot second and I think what would remain would still be a strong, successful woman. I am not thankful for my mental illness because it does me more harm than good. I don't want to give it any props. No accolades, no applause, no misty-eyed celebratory speeches. I understand that most mental health narratives aren't celebrating illness, they're celebrating the self, but I'm always concerned when these stories seem to channel the unhealthy idea that potential is defined by disease—i.e. our perception of our bipolar poster boy Van Gogh and the role his illness played in "inspiring" his genius.

Van Gogh was a masterful artist who was thought to have bipolar disorder. He was also a whiny jagoff with a taste for lead paint and absinthe. For complete transparency, I am very whiny too—however, I prefer medical marijuana over licking my lead-tainted walls—and I'd like to think that I'm a talented writer. According to the goals I've set for myself in regards to accruing readers and publishing pieces, I'm definitely tapping into my potential. Not only is writing something I'm good at, but being a writer is an integral component of my identity. But something that is not lost on me is that the bulk of my writing focuses on sharing my life with bipolar disorder. (You're probably already aware of this considering you're reading this. P.S. Thanks for that!) Van Gogh is to brush strokes as I am to key clicking (and yes, I realize I'm comparing my talents to Van Gogh, but I'm having a great self-esteem day so leave me alone). Writing is an outlet, it keeps me healthy, it gives me power, but if I had to choose between illness and outlet, I wish I had nothing to write about! I'm just kidding, I know I'd still write about other things. For instance, I could finally finish my screenplay, *Midnight in the Garden of Good and Weevil*, about a young beetle with a passion for investigative reporting and laying larvae in Spanish moss. Anyway, my bipolar disorder doesn't make me a better writer. I just write about it because it's a part of my life that I need to process. CliffsNotes: being a writer is part of my identity, having bipolar is not.

But here's the thing: the reality is that my bipolar is not going away. I'm completely aware that it's a chronic illness that I'll always have to live with and manage. It's a perpetual up and down, side to side, too high or too low. It's all about pushing past the rough times and dedicating my life to the pursuit of balance. I've had to learn how to take care of myself, which means understanding my illness, finding the language to talk about it, and figuring out how to achieve my goals despite my shitty brain chemistry. That's been a significant part of my journey and I'll always have these challenges. I cope by doing everything in my power to de-glamorize my illness, to take it out of the spotlight, to value myself by focusing on my accomplishments, not as someone with bipolar but as the kickass bitch that I am. Disorder takes a backseat.

I think many mental health narratives embrace life with an illness because it's a great way to cope. Your illness isn't going anywhere. It's a roommate you can't evict so you learn to live around it. You just have to make it work and hope that your roomie doesn't light your house on fire. Acceptance is an essential step toward ownership of illness. And as I read the stories of others living with mental illness during Mental Health Awareness Month, I appreciate their honesty and their passion. We need to raise our voices and share who we are, talk about what we go through. If we all keep talking about mental illness, stigma doesn't stand a chance.

Here's my own story using my own words:

Hi, I'm Rachel.
I don't thank my bipolar.
For anything.
Not a single thing.
I acknowledge my illness, I understand it, I make my peace, but I don't give my bipolar any credit. That belongs to me.
With or without it, I'm fabulous.
And my mental illness can go fuck itself.

my voice

I am defending my dissertation in a week. Between now and 10:30 a.m. on February 23, 2017, my schedule is completely packed:

1) I have to actually finish my academic spiel. How do you slap two-hundred pages onto a PowerPoint presentation anyway? Can I use Word Art? *Ack.*

2) Next, I have to practice and time the damn thing so I'm at thirty minutes—no more, no less—which seems nearly impossible. Every time I think about it, my palms instantly get sweaty and the lump in my throat bulges. *Blurgh.*

3) I also have to make sure that I triumphantly champion this dissertation with the courage and conviction of an impenetrable Elizabeth Warren yelling at the Senate. To be that confident, that collected. *Swoon.* Honestly, I know what I'm talking about, but understandably, I still kind of feel like puking. (Does Elizabeth Warren even puke?)

This is the pinnacle of my educational existence. The degree, the title, more importantly: the cool octagon hat. I don't want to fuck this up. I want to believe that I can make this happen. I've been doing this work for years. I'm passionate and I've got a solid work ethic.

I'm so close.

If it wasn't for the auditory hallucinations, I'd be a sure thing. When you experience a psychotic depression, it is not uncommon to have auditory hallucinations. Your brain cracks in half, and in addition to the festering stew of tears, delusions, fear, paranoia, anxiety, and utter hopelessness that gushes out, occasionally you can find trace amounts of "hearing things" mixed in. I've lived with bipolar for about fifteen years, and this is the first time I've had auditory hallucinations.

My disease learned a new trick. *Yeeeeeeah*. At my appointment this afternoon, my psychiatrist told me that since the voice in my head isn't frightening (other than the fact that, ya know, I'm hearing a fucking voice), it's not trying to convince me that I'm a terrible, shitty person, and it's not demanding me to do anything, that I just have to sit with the voice, try my best to ignore the voice, and let the voice fade into a whisper. There's no medication on the market manufactured specifically to eradicate extra voices in your head. If your current antipsychotics aren't taking them down, that means you have to move on to another brand of crazy-stabilizers.

My brain chemistry is shifting. Words all good bipolars dread hearing. It means retreating back to the rigged game of pharmaceutical hide and seek. Assessing if the terrible side effects from the meds are worth the dulling of your disorder's symptoms. It is a particularly cruel sentencing. Pack up your pill bottles and titrate off the old guard because it's time to clean out the medicine cabinet and invite some new prescriptions into your life. The process is daunting. Emotionally exhausting. Taxing on your body. It honestly feels like a gut-wrenching break up. The meds that worked - well, used to work - the meds that you trusted, that you relied on to keep your head together - well, used to - the meds that took you so long to find, are now obsolete. Start again. Game over. *Fuck*.

But the problem is, I can't start yet. I can't introduce a brand new, wild card psychiatric med that could potentially trash my skull. Instead, I have to push through this week, prepare and defend, wait patiently for the new script, and entertain the voice in my head until February 24th. Only then can the barrage of new meds on my brain begin.

The PowerPoint, the time limit, the confidence, the research, that's all me. That's what I've been dedicating my life to. I see myself in the work. I am the work. I'm proud of how far I've come. But I am also crazy.

Bipolar is nothing new, but this voice is. And while it destroys me to think that there's a good chance I'll be standing in front of my committee defending my work while simultaneously pretending to be sane, it also makes me feel doubly proud of how far I've come. *I'm crushing it.* And soon, I'll be the proud owner of a kickass velvet hat.

a message to my meds

Dear lithium, Seroquel, Lamictal, Zoloft (as needed), Ativan (as needed), and Klonopin (as needed),

What can I say? We've had a lot of good times and a lot of tough times together. Zoloft, remember that time when you spiked my mania and I couldn't subdue my sparkly, agitated mind, so I ended up only drinking bubble tea for four days because I thought I was too beautiful to need food?

Lamictal, you sure can slow me down. Remember that time my brain chemistry was still adjusting to your increased dose and I had to cancel my meetings for an entire week because I couldn't manage to rub two brain cells together under the weight of your cognitive fog?

Hey, do yinz remember all those times when you completely stopped working and I lost my mind? Like when I plateaued on Seroquel, became psychotically depressed, and saw spiders? Or that time I became so full-blown manic, I drew all over myself with Crayola markers because I thought I was a kaleidoscope?

We sure do share a lot of memories!

To be honest, it hasn't always been easy between us. At times, I've loathed you. I've felt trapped by you. You patched me up, but made me feel broken at the same time. I guess you can say that our relationship has always been complicated.

But the truth is, I have to thank you all. My pharmaceutical posse, you've made a lot possible. You've empowered me to pursue my goals, you've enabled me to have healthy relationships with friends, family, and myself, and you have provided me a means of control that I've sorely needed because - as we both know - bipolar disorder never goes away.

These past few years have been particularly difficult—with the routine struggles that come from mental illness, the instances when you guys stopped pulling your weight, and with the stress of pursuing a doctoral degree—keeping my head above water wasn't exactly an easy task.

So I'm thrilled to announce that last Thursday I successfully defended my dissertation! I'm a doctor! I couldn't have done it without you guys. With your support and guidance, I've learned how to own my illness, how to ask for help when I'm struggling with stability, and that there is hope. When I take you guys, I can sleep, I can eat, I can work, I can go to school, I can function. You empower me to be who I truly am—someone who is ambitious, capable, smart, funny—a woman who loves life, even with this disease.

I just - I never thought I'd get here. I'm a doctor, I'm the healthiest I've ever been, both emotionally and physically, and most importantly, I've learned to love myself, illness and all. I think the reason I was able to do it is because I didn't have to do it alone. My husband, family, friends, pets, therapist, psychiatrist, and you six have always been there for me, by my side, in my heart, and in my brain—and I've grown to be a person who I'm immensely proud of.

I talk about my life with bipolar disorder so often because it is important to challenge how we think about mental illness - the stigma, the prejudice, the limitations we impose when we label. And most importantly, challenge how we think about the people who struggle with these illnesses, myself included. Over the years, I've confronted the negative perceptions I have about myself, challenged the self stigma I've carried with me for so long, learned how to forgive myself when I make mistakes, celebrated my accomplishments without being clouded by doubt, and embraced the fact that I'm worth it.

I know we've had our disagreements and falling outs, you guys haven't always been easy to live with, but I'm thankful for the power you've given me.

I'm thankful for the hope.

We're not always going to get along, but I couldn't do it without you.

Let's both keep up the good work,
Dr. Rach

early thirties

My friends are having babies
or they already have a baby or two with a vasectomy penciled in on the calendar,
tiny little likenesses,
and they smile for photos just like happy families are supposed to
with captions that read "Baby's first anything"
and "I've never been so tired and so happy in my life,"
posts dedicated to the earnest discussion of bodily fluids and the documentation of tantrums,
written with a survivalist sense of humor and tacked up all over social media.
I sit back and sigh
on a couch in a living room that is nowhere near childproof,
comforted by the tumbleweeds ambling about in my womb.
I love children and my friends' sweet, squirmy little ones,
but I would never want a baby like me,
with my kind of crazy.
This doesn't make me sad. That's just how it is.
So, here I am, defining my life differently,
sleeping in and eating candy corn for dinner,
four pets that have my eyes and no need for college tuition,
my life is full.

I am happy to be a baby bystander.

have eating disorder, will travel

I just got home from Vegas. My husband and I trekked through the chilly Pittsburgh airport, triumphantly remembered where we parked our car, hit the road for home, and now I'm nestled comfortably on the couch in between two snoring dogs, sans bra. I've only just posted "I'm happy to be in you, Pgh" on Facebook and people have messaged me about where we're going next. Everybody loves to travel, right?

Except me. Well, that is until recently. For most of my life, I've harbored the very unpopular opinion that traveling is *the worst* - a fact that always felt embarrassing to admit, like it was some kind of character flaw. Here's the thing. Talking about traveling is like talking about the weather. Most people agree that sun is better than rain, and traveling is better than staying at home.

"I would love to travel more."

"I've been to XYZ and I want to go to Q."

"We're saving money for a month-long trip to Who Knows Where."

These are commonly uttered phrases. Most people love to travel almost as much as they love to talk about traveling. But honestly, I always felt that "loving traveling" was a super canned response. Just like saying you're "fine" when you just ran over your cat. It's easier to say you enjoy gallivanting all over the globe than defend why you're a homebody. That said, I think it's fair to say that not liking travel is definitely the minority mindset. Most people love to submit to their wanderlust and snap Instagram photos of trips taken, friends met, and meals eaten all over the world.

I've always hated flying (still do) and, for many years, I would say that I love the destination, just hate the transportation, even though that was a bit of a lie. Yes, destinations are wonderful and most people do not like running around an airport, pinning their hopes and dreams on a shitty airline running its planes on time. Yes, most people agree that the to and fro is rarely the fun part. I'm not alone on that one. But up until somewhat recently, I didn't like traveling OR the destination, and I have my reasons. Both 1) cause anxiety, 2) disrupt my routine, 3) mess with my sleep, and 4) most importantly, fuck with my meal planning. I guess I forgot to mention a critical detail—it's not a character flaw, but it's something that heavily impacts how I experience life—I have a history of disordered eating. And living with an eating disorder not only makes everyday life a challenge, but can make traveling a nightmare. I've been all over the spectrum of disordered eating, and while I don't have many stamps in my passport, I do have a long rap sheet chronicling doctor's visits, capturing the sights, smells, and sounds of hospitals, and documenting the copious amount of exotic medication I've consumed throughout my lifetime.

I was partly raised by my eating disorders. Anorexia slinked inside me during my early teen years. She started out harmless enough, encouraging me to eat healthy and exercise, but my knack for abiding by my unrelenting discipline combined with anorexia's ruthlessness had grave consequences. For starters, it resulted in losing too much weight too quickly and everyone staring at my hip bones. And my clavicle. And my pinched shoulders. And my ribs. While, at first, I felt attractive and anorexia gave me this false sense of control, my eating disorder quickly gained momentum and set its sights on destroying me. It was the opposite of a feeding frenzy. It was a starving frenzy. I couldn't eat anymore. I felt embarrassed of my bones, of fainting in German class, of scaring my friends and family. But eating seemed impossible.

You might not believe me, but my hand wouldn't obey the command to lift a strawberry from my plate into my mouth. My mouth wouldn't close. My teeth wouldn't chew. And I definitely wouldn't swallow. It pains me to remember the Great Strawberry Fight of 2002. My parents sitting with me at the dinner table begging me to eat a bowl of strawberries - my favorite - and their surprise that I could say I wanted them, cry because I wanted them, and yet not eat them. They didn't understand. And neither did I, really. I just didn't know how to eat. My junior year of high school, I was supposed to go to Germany but my teachers didn't want me to because I was a skeleton who couldn't conjugate verbs. Even if they had agreed to take me, my parents would've refused to send me since they were pretty sure that I'd restrict even more in a foreign country with foreign foods—I was already about to die on American soil as it was. I stayed stateside, waiting to die, but luckily, my family and friends wouldn't hand me over to my eating disorder without a fight. They gave me hope, and after a lot of hard work and therapy, I started eating strawberries again.

Recovery is a bitch, and for most people struggling with eating disorders, it takes between three and seven years to drag yourself toward the light at the end of the tunnel (I blame it partially on low bone density #anorexiahumor), and then comes a lifetime of management (you have to pardon my gallows humor because eating disorders are incredibly serious - in fact, they have the highest mortality rate of any psychiatric illness). In my case, after seven years (right on schedule!) of fighting this disease, I started to get better, to eat and heal and go to therapy and take medication for my bipolar disorder (comorbidity is also a bitch). I managed to escape anorexia and evade her plan of starving me to death, but I couldn't completely get rid of her. To this day, she's still in earshot, but I try my best not to listen, not to lose myself, and not give in to her demands. It's not easy, but her voice has gotten quieter over the years.

Unfortunately, I didn't lose the looming presence of an eating disorder. It just took a different form. Introducing binge eating disorder. Binge eating disorder was like this terrible friend that tagged along everywhere, pestering me about my food choices and making judgmental comments about my weight, but I just couldn't shake her because I worried that no one else would put up with me since I was getting fat. Even though I wasn't anorexic, I still didn't know how to eat—if I wasn't restricting, what was I supposed to do?—so I let my binge eating disorder take over. I went from extreme starving to extreme eating. Over the course of ten years, I went from 98 pounds to 260 pounds and everywhere in between. Lots of ups and downs, lots of strain on my body, lots of agony and anxiety, and lots of disruption in my life. Eventually, my brain and body caved to binge eating disorder's peer pressure and my sense of self-worth was completely non-existent. My family took a trip to Spain, but I told them I couldn't go because I was afraid of eating abroad, of not fitting in the airplane seat, of being a fat tourist. I was consumed by the fear that people who hailed from all over the world would watch me eat, shaking their heads with disgust, mumbling in different languages. I chose to stay home.

For years, traveling meant having to figure out a whole new system to eat without gaining weight, without fainting, and still feel in control. And it wasn't exactly portable because different places had different types of food. When you travel, there is no guarantee that you'll have access to your "safe foods"—foods that you have categorized as being "okay to eat" based on your own, individualized criteria. Examples: foods that you feel comfortable eating since you know the exact number of calories, foods that are easy to puke up if you need to pull the trigger, foods that provide some form of comfort. You get the idea.

Personally, my eating disorders make me very brand loyal. I've had some terrifying experiences where I can't find MY brand of peanut butter (Jif reduced fat creamy) and it honestly feels like the end of the world (that's mental illness for ya). The only bread I like is Arnold's 12 Grain Wheat Bread and that isn't available in every state. Actually, in Virginia, it's sold under the name Brownberry - same bread, different name. We crazies do our homework because most of us can't eat food we don't understand, that isn't familiar, because that food may contain the secret ingredient to make us blow up like a balloon, to make us lose control. We pack a carry-on suitcase with safe foods because, ultimately, food is dangerous and you want to keep your enemy as close as possible, like a jar of Jif you keep in the center console of your car.

Traveling is a challenge because there are a lot of unexpected, exciting twists and turns—the things most people like about a vacation—but for people living with eating disorders, it can feel more like a stint on a battlefield. For so long, even the idea of a vacation just put me on high alert. Vacations were exhausting, anxiety provoking, only semi-rewarding and, in many ways, not really worth it. My mindset for years was that I'll stay home with my dogs, my peanut butter, and my bread, thanks. It's a societal expectation to say you love to travel and even more so to follow through, but for a long while, I was just like, "Fuck it." Sanity meant a staycation.

But I just got home from Vegas. This past October, I went to Seattle. Last summer, I went to the Outer Banks. Two years ago, I went to Zurich and Paris. I've learned how to manage my eating disorder (and my bipolar disorder - they're all related in this incestuous fuck fest called being mentally ill) and, subsequently, I've become braver and more willing to try new things, like travel. To go to different locations where I might have to eat at a restaurant for two meals on the same day (scary!) and I might have to try new foods. I have to go in blind of any caloric intel. I have to practice eating and enjoying it, which for me, was a relatively successful "fake it till you make it" style approach. And I'm happy to say I've gotten so much better. I eat and work hard to make sure I don't undereat. Or overeat. I make mistakes and remind myself to be kind afterwards. I'm buying airplane tickets and finding that I do fit in the seat (and even if I didn't, who cares!). I've made peace with my body and I know how to feed it. These days, I care more about being brave and having enough energy to take on new adventures.

So, here I am. My dogs are farting blissfully and doing that cute dog dreamy thing where they wiggle their paws as they run in their sleep, and I'm writing this as I simultaneously post Vegas photos on my Instagram: me vaping in front of Hermes at midnight, me trying In-N-Out Burger for the first time, me wearing a tight sequin dress and potentially catastrophic heels out to a club, me eating a chocolate cupcake from the Bellagio's patisserie, the usual. And I feel accomplished. And content. I traveled and I enjoyed it - like everyone else seems to - and while I'm happy to be home, I'm not resigned to stay still forever. "We should go to Vancouver," my husband says as he closes his book and rests next to me on the couch. And I can't help but smile because I know I will. Because I know I can do it. Because I want to.

madness:
a story told through handbags

Kate Spade, acclaimed fashion designer, businesswoman, and trendsetter, died by suicide on June 5, 2018. As someone with a love for handbags and a hatred of mental illness, her death has been on my mind. My twenty-year relationship with bags isn't just a materialistic hobby, it's something tangled up in my life that helps me tell a story of growing up and figuring things out. My history with handbags provides a timeline of my life with mental illness. I write this in memory of Kate.

I love handbags. Wait, no, that's not right. I L-O-O-O-O-V-E handbags. In this life, we all have to pick our poison, and mine's Prada. And Louis Vuitton. And Marc Jacobs. And Tory Burch. And Coach. And Kate Spade. You get the idea. Since high school, I have had an infatuation with handbags, and while my foray into purses started out with a handmade bag repurposed from an old pair of jean shorts (fondly referred to as my "ass bag"—I've always had a way with words), it eventually grew to include a diverse collection of designer brands. Handbags always appealed to me because they were a way to dress up an outfit, to look put together and polished, even if you're wearing sweatpants. Purses have always been a way to level up my fashion game because, admittedly, I dress like a combination of a nerdy high schooler from the late '00s mixed with a middle-aged divorcee on a domestic cruise. Let's just put it this way: I have twelve sloth t-shirts, three *Clueless* t-shirts, five pairs of boat shoes, animal print everything, and I've never met a sequin I didn't like. The numbers add up. I've never really cultivated a unique sense of style, instead opting for graphic tees and sparkly shoes, but I've always felt that carrying a fancy bag is the ultimate accessory. Purses have always served a purpose in my life.

It all starts where most problems start: high school. If I had to describe my high school experience in five words, they would be: perfectionism, spaghetti string tank tops, amazing friends, Dave Matthews Band obsession, bipolar disorder, and anorexia. And not being able to count (I know that's way more than five words, but I'm not a perfectionist anymore!). My struggle with anorexia was pretty severe and I had many touch and go moments during my four years trapped in high school. I was hungry to be thin - no, I was ravenous. Being thin meant being lovable, and I found perfection quantified by the numbers on my scale. If I was skinny enough, I'd be worthwhile. I found validation with the size of my jeans. Controlling my eating was a way to control my life, which, at the time, felt chaotic and unpredictable (thanks bipolar #foreshadowing).

While I began dabbling in disordered eating my freshman year of high school, I dove head first into anorexia when I was diagnosed with bipolar disorder my junior year. I had been struggling secretly with bipolar since I was fifteen, but after a hard to ignore manic episode, my bipolar suddenly became visible. I was seventeen when I was schlepped off to the psychiatrist's office and formerly diagnosed with bipolar disorder. With "bipolar" now emblazoned on my forehead, I found some comfort knowing my experience had a name, but the momentary relief the label provided was overshadowed by feelings of intense shame. I tightened my grip on my anorexia as a way to feel in control, but really, anorexia tightened its grip on me. I was perpetually empty and in agony but I refused to recognize my anorexia and my bipolar as being conditions I needed to treat. I didn't want to go to therapy, take my meds, eat food, or stop exercising because that would confirm that I was, in fact, crazy. To me, crazy meant isolation, it meant being a failure, being unloved, being forgotten. During the worst periods of my illness, it wasn't that I wanted to die exactly, but I didn't know how to live anymore. My existence was consumed by mental illness. My parents braced themselves for the day that I wouldn't wake up. I closed my eyes every night praying that I'd wake up cured or I wouldn't wake up at all. I saw myself as being too broken to ever get better. (The bag bit is around the bend, be patient!)

I managed to graduate high school with a 4.2 GPA and a visible rib cage, and I desperately wanted to go to college and have the opportunity to start over. My parents were reluctant to let me go considering how sick I was, but my desire to leave my hometown with the hope of finding myself on a college campus was a huge motivator for me to try and take my life back. The summer before college, I committed to eating so my parents would sign off on me going to school. I showed my parents that I could manage my care and they agreed to let me go to college. I'd like to say that I went away to college and became an empowered young woman who looked adversity in the face and laughed, refusing to let illness be her legacy, and instead, lived her life, took her meds, and challenged her feelings of worthlessness, but I still struggled. These were big problems that weren't going to just go away. I moved into my dorm room in late August and I was the happiest I've ever been. But while I felt euphoric, I was actually just as sick as before. The manifestation of my illness had mutated, but my bipolar was just as vicious - just sparklier.

My college years were some of the best years of my life for a few reasons: 1) I love learning so I found a safehaven in my classes. Education gave me the opportunity to excel. To grow and define myself as a smart and ambitious person. I didn't have to be sick. I could be successful. 2) I made some truly incredible friends and had the opportunity to interact with different types of people with diverse ideas that were vastly different from my own experiences growing up. 3) I started dating my husband who helped me learn how to love myself as I am and not how I thought I should be. 4) I had a lot of sex, I went to a lot of parties, and I did a lot of drugs—not necessarily a great idea but, you know, typical endearing college shenanigans (okay, actually more dangerous than endearing). 5) I let my mania take over. Bipolar disorder convinced me that it was my friend, not a source of suffering. Back then, manic me felt like the real me - the best version of me - so I let my bipolar infiltrate how I thought about myself and manipulate how I interacted with the world. I did some very dumb and risky things, but due to my privilege as a white woman with a supportive family and access to resources, I always ended up okay. I don't think I understood how lucky I really was until much later in my life. I would stumble and fall and the people in my life would pick me back up again, no questions asked. Yes, I was resilient, but I was also incredibly privileged. It's important to make that distinction. Most people living with mental illnesses do not have the same luxuries that I had growing up (and still do). The trajectory of my life was impacted by illness but not entirely sabotaged. Plus, in college, I started eating again. Not necessarily reliably, but I made the effort. I was having way too much fun to die.

My ass bag served me well during college (see, I told you we'd come back to bags!). I covered it in buttons that advertised how liberal and edgy I thought I was, plus I could hide weed in between the lining. It made a statement and was very practical. I wore sparkly shoes and loudly colored tops with my ass bag slung over my shoulder. I was hot shit. But after graduating from college, I decided I needed to refine my image and I hung my ass bag in the closet and started paying attention to designer brands that were way out of my reach. I craved to look stylish and sophisticated. But as a psychology major graduating in 2007, I found myself with few lucrative job prospects. Thanks a lot, Freud! Thanks a lot, tanking economy! Unfortunately, no fashion house would take my IOUs. Not wanting to move back home, I left Arlington, Virginia and made the trek to Pittsburgh to be with my then boyfriend (now husband). He was a computer science major who did not share in my struggles of finding a job. Our society sure does love zeroes and ones and the people who click the keys. We lived in an apartment with another couple, and I saved what I could so I could buy Coach and Kate Spade handbags. I remember justifying some of these purchases by saying they were "investments," even though my boyfriend was not shy to point out that I never sold any of them for more than I purchased them, so it didn't really seem like a smart way to handle my money. Louis Vuitton would not help me pad my 401k. But I did it anyway because handbags made me happy.

My life in Pittsburgh wasn't just the start of being painfully cold in the winters, putting French fries on my salads and sandwiches, and buying handbags, it was also the first time in my life I decided to explore my identity as someone living with a mental illness. Admitting it for real this time and owning it. I realized that my manic lifestyle was not sustainable anymore since I needed a job and couldn't afford to dive off the deep end every couple of months. For the first time ever, I started actually taking my meds - and as prescribed (ooooh, ahhhh) - and for the first time ever, I found stability (what a coinkydink!). I didn't do drugs, I muffled my ears to mania's siren song, and I was able to hold down a job and not fall apart. I felt in control for the first time. Well, for the first time in my life. I didn't think this was possible, yet here I was. The only downside was that I was fat.

So what does this have to do with handbags? I'm getting there. A lot of psychiatric medications fuck with your metabolism. I went from being a crazy skinny girl to being a fat stable girl, and while I celebrated the fact that I was a responsible adult, the anorexic voice in my head wouldn't stop admonishing me for being weak and overweight. It was incredibly hard trying to stay healthy while my inner disordered eating monologue told me I was quickly sinking into new depths of disgusting. I kept getting fatter, and soon none of my clothes fit. Soon, I was more self-conscious than ever. I felt dumpy and blubbery and embarrassed of how much space I took up. I also felt conflicted and confused. I wanted to be stable and sane, but I equally wanted to be skinny—why were the two mutually exclusive? Was it really one or the other? I threw away my scale that kept scolding me, and I bought jeans and cried at the size on the tags.

But I didn't throw in the towel (and I'm not talking a hand towel, like a large towel, come on, I'm like two-hundred pounds, be realistic). I didn't stop taking my meds or stop eating. I knew that I deserved to be happy, which meant I needed to take care of myself. This was a HUGE accomplishment for me. Anyone who has struggled with body image (which is, like, totally everyone) can understand how empowering it is to take back and rewrite your narrative. After quite a bit of troubleshooting, I finally found a way to walk around the world in my fat body. What was my secret? I obscured my belly with a fancy handbag! Bags were a distraction, and I started buying expensive bags to hide behind. Givenchy decoys for the win! Purses became camouflage. I could find refuge behind a large Marc Jacobs handbag. People would look at the bag and not at my body. The fancier the bag, the better. Chanel offered fat girl salvation. If I looked rich then maybe people wouldn't care that I was fat. When I was freshly fat, all I wanted to do was blend in, to fade into the background. I didn't want to stick out. But I learned that sporting a Louis Vuitton on my arm made me stand out for what I thought were the right reasons. I wasn't a chubby eyesore; I was a chubby girl rocking a $2,000 purse. I could live with that. And you can, too! (Just kidding, that is ridiculously way too much for a bag! Oh, the follies of youth! And madness, can't forget that #foreshadowing).

Reality check. Did I have $2,000 to throw around? Nope! (Remember, psych major and poor economy). Did that stop me? Nope! I struggled to afford my extravagant purse lifestyle, and I eventually gave up and focused on paying everything off. *Smart move, Rach!* Well, that was up until my meds stopped working. Okay, so here's the thing with mental illnesses and meds: meds are not a cure. They are a tool that help you manage your illness, but taking medication doesn't mean you won't experience symptoms. For many people, meds just mute their illness. And taking your meds doesn't guarantee you will be able to manage things forever. It is very possible that you could plateau on your medication. They work for a while, but your body adjusts and your chemistry shifts, especially if you have environmental stressors, and then they become less effective. And it can happen pretty slowly—so slowly that you might not even notice that you're going crazy. That's what happened to me.

I was taking my meds religiously so I didn't think anything could go wrong. I didn't recognize the mania creeping in. I didn't see the signs of madness scratching at my brain. I didn't realize that my thoughts were becoming fevered and fractured. I smiled as I swallowed my lithium and didn't detect that I was neck deep in bipolar quicksand. My husband refers to 2009 as the "year of the handbag," which is fitting considering that year I went absolutely bat shit and bought a shit ton of designer handbags. When you are hypomanic/manic, every idea is a brilliant idea. Bags really did seem like investments. Luxury handbags became a very logical uniform. Bags were my ticket into being a desirable person. *Who needs to pay rent, amiright?* I blew threw money without even blinking. And here is a great example of where my privilege comes into play. After my year-long shopping spree, my credit card statement revealed that something was wrong and I needed help. My family intervened and my boyfriend and parents were able to help me claw out of the hole. My psychiatrist figured out a new cocktail of meds to level me out. I was very, very lucky. I got back on track and still had a closet full of purses. I was also still fat, but that no longer seemed like that big of a deal. I just wanted to be me and not my disease.

I'm still fat, and I'm happy to report that I'm not my illnesses. While my anorexic, bipolar, and fat-fueled adventure isn't over - these illnesses will always be a force in my life that I need to fight - I am better. And though my relationship with purses has always been somewhat extreme (extremes are what bipolar people do best), they still hold a place in my heart. For years, purses were an outlet for self-expression. They helped me sift through my identity. They helped me cope with my mental illness and negotiate my fatness. They were a source of confidence. I don't really buy bags anymore and I realize that material possessions don't make you a better person, but, I admit, on a bad self-esteem day, I am not above rocking a Burberry to give me the boost I need. We all have our vices. My bags didn't make me better, but they helped me stop berating myself. They gave me space to learn how to be myself and exist in a world that shuns both fat people and crazy people. Was it the best means of coping? Not really, but it worked for me at the time. For better or for worse, Alexander Wang helped me do the damn thang.

In my own story, purses have been a source of comfort that offered a sense of belonging, and as I've been reading about Spade's energy and excitement about building her empire, I can't help but wonder what we didn't know. Hell, I just look like a fat chick with a Dooney and Bourke; people see the image, not the illness. I don't know what she was going through, what was going through her head, and no one will probably ever really know. The image we project isn't reflective of who we really are. It doesn't tell the majority of our story. We let society see what we want it to see and the rest is tucked away. Behind clothes. Behind cars. Behind houses. Behind handbags. Yesterday, I used a Kate Spade bag and I couldn't help but think about my own suicide attempts. I thought about my life with mental illness and the experiences I've had thus far trying to live in my skin. How, for me, as silly as this sounds, part of my journey has been told through my relationship with handbags. As a crazy woman, as a fat woman, as someone figuring out how she fits in the world. My heart hurts for Kate Spade and her family, and I thank her for the joy she provided me with her designs. Pebbled leather handbags in bright colors with terrific hardware and top quality stitching have never cured anything for anyone, but they did provide something I needed during different parts of my life. What's that quote? "Everyone you meet is fighting a battle you know nothing about. Be kind. Always." And be honest with yourself and ask for help when you need it.

Thanks for helping me feel seen. We'll miss you, Kate.

Guess what!

My psychiatrist lowered my dose of antipsychotics!

This may seem like a weird fact to advertise, an odd event to celebrate, and a bizarre thing to brag about, but this is a big fucking deal. Because this means I've been impressively stable! Kudos to my brain for behaving. And a shoutout to solid sleep. I couldn't have done it without you, therapist! Here's looking at you, psychiatrist. Props to my husband for all of the love and support. And lastly, I want to thank all of the supporting players who helped make this possible: friends, family, the movie *Clueless*, chocolate, my pets, exercise, medical marijuana, body positive Insta accounts, Diego Luna, and sunshine. Wow, we finally did it, team! I'll never forget any of you!

I'm so happy that I'm on a lowered dose of Seroquel, but I have to pause for a quick dose of reality: I know I won't be stable forever. Bipolar disorder just doesn't work that way. The nature of the illness is mercilessly batting you back and forth between depression and mania, with pit stops in hypomania and wrong turns into psychosis. The illness isn't static. It's fluid and unpredictable. Mental illness is not a linear adventure. You fight, you fall apart, you struggle, you succeed. To and fro, up and down, side to side, it's a bumpy ride. But that doesn't mean you can't control certain aspects of your illness. That doesn't mean you won't have periods of your life where you can live well because your illness lays low. It can be subdued by hard work and dedicated effort. Focusing on what needs to happen in order to calibrate a bipolar brain—to coax it into compliance and keep it cooperative. Exercising, eating right, sleeping, and being proactive when it comes to dodging triggers and managing stress. You can do it, #inspirationalpinterestquote (but seriously, you can)!

Yes, some days are better than others—okay, let's be real here, some weeks, some months, some years are better than others—but you can't give up. You can't stop doing what it takes, pushing and practicing, reaching for balance. Commit to the hard work because you deserve to be healthy. And when you finally get there, while you might not stay for long, pat yourself on the back because, for now, you've done it. Take a bow, beam at the crowd, and pose with your bouquet. You deserve to be proud. Take it from me, a fellow crazy person with a history of bad decisions and a taste for the spotlight. Bravo!

Right now, I'm proud of myself! Way to go, me! It's all about Rachel! At this very moment, due to my effort and diligence, things are balanced and I have the tools to help me stay this way for as long as possible. So, what does this mean for me? This means less cognitive fog, less dehydration, my metabolism gets a bit of a break, and I can stretch my prescriptions further (for the inquisitive reader, check out more gruesome details at Web-MD ooooh, aaaah)! I'm all about that bonkers bargain. Slide me those generics, plz. My pill cutter is at the ready, eagerly anticipating cutting my pills into pieces since I was promoted from 800 mg to 750 mg (don't be deceived by the amount—this 50 mg difference is a big deal). Woohoo! It's really affirming to palm fewer pills every night; to choke down fewer chalky tablets that leave a gritty residue on the back of your tongue. It's a tangible sign that I'm making progress. It's been slow and I know I'll inevitably slip, because even when you do everything "right," you're not impervious to a persistent illness, but, for right now, bipolar disorder is working for ME! This mood disorder is muted and it's because I'm tough as fuck. *Please, please, quiet your applause.*

I understand that you might find all of this hard to believe. Celebrating this small reduction in medication might not make sense to you. You still see a lot of prescription bottles perched in my medicine cabinet and you might think this victory is ridiculous. But my faith in myself is not displaced. I do my best to stay optimistic and hopeful, which means taking credit for these pharmaceutical accomplishments. But truthfully, it's not just about swallowing fewer tablets, it's about not giving up. This is a big deal and I'm so proud. I've worked really hard to get here and I'm confident that I'll be able to get here again after things get shaky. But for now, I'll enjoy it while it lasts.

family history of

...

Very few people like going to the doctor, but I absolutely LOATHE it. Mostly due to my unfortunate collection of condemning diagnoses glued together by colorful, clinically quantifiable experiences. It doesn't help that I am a woman either. Boo.

Without fail, my doctor starts out with a gentle but serious smile, attentive head nods, and sticks to the *respectful clinician* script:

"I'm Dr. Y, nice to meet you."

"What brought you here today?"

"Oh, okay, I see. Let's take a look, shall we?"

But as soon as that chart is cracked open, revealing "anorexia" and "bipolar I," slapped visibly on the top, I lose all credibility as a person. I mean patient. Nah, I really mean both.

"Does your psychiatrist know you're here?"

"What does your therapist say about all this?"

"Hmmm. That's a lot of meds."

Ugh. Dr. Y, are you going to do your job or not?

The presenting problem is dismissed, the condescending "uh-huh's" exponentially increase, and without fail, I'm instructed to tell my psychiatrist to check my levels, screen for toxicity in my blood stream – I mean, what is that liver of mine up to these days? My meds must be out of whack.

Just stop.

My psychiatrist is competent but, more importantly, we work well together. I advocate, I ask for help, I understand my symptoms. I communicate with the ease of someone who has been mentally ill since fifteen.

Don't avoid me by deferring to my psychiatrist.

After these visits, I remind myself that this isn't actually about my meds or the wherewithal of my psychiatrist. It isn't just about me. I'm bearing the brunt of it, but this is stigma in action. And stigma has the tendency to fuck with my life. In the examination room, in the classroom, during the interview, as I reach for my insurance card. My diagnoses tend to be the first thing the system sees.

Dear podiatrist, physical therapist, gastroenterologist, orthopedic surgeon, to my primary care physician and all the nurses in her practice, don't ignore me. Please, hear me. My mental illness doesn't undermine the fact that I get sick. Mental illness doesn't make me immune to the flu, kidney infections, mono, ulcers, allergic reactions, and all the things that bring all people into the waiting room.

I schedule my appointments with a deep breath. *I am not imaginary.*

Dear doctors, stop focusing on the parts of me listed in the DSM because all of me is in your office asking to be seen.

world bipolar day:
why do we care so much
about vincent van gogh?

March 30th is World Bipolar Day, and it's no accident that this date falls on Vincent van Gogh's birthday. Van Gogh, the undisputedly revered and gifted artist who endured a turbulent, unhappy, and erratic existence, was posthumously diagnosed with bipolar disorder based on the nature of his struggles, his eccentricities, and documented behaviors. Van Gogh is often regarded as the patron saint of bipolar disorder, but before I grab my *The Starry Night* tote bag, I want to dig into his story and then rant a lot. Spoiler alert, I'm not his biggest fan.

Background for those who are unfamiliar with van Gogh:

By all accounts, van Gogh had a relatively shitty life. His childhood was less than stellar and he felt misplaced and isolated a good chunk of the time. As an adult, he struggled finding a career that would stick. First, he apprenticed as an art dealer, and then for a period, he embraced his growing religious fervor and dedicated his life to becoming a man of God. He became an evangelical preacher with bouts of depression who was ultimately booted from his church, and then he shifted his attention and energy towards agnosticism, socialist ideology, and art. When it came to social skills, he made quite the reputation as an entitled jerk that pulled out his stalker moves when he was "friend zoned." Sarcastic sorry, van Bro-gh. Anyway, according to Blumer (2002), as van Gogh's artistic career developed, he began experiencing episodic bursts of terror, physical pain, and lapses of consciousness. Not to mention, he really liked to pound the absinthe and down the frequent cognac or two. As an adult, van Gogh grew increasingly volatile, untidy, quarrelsome, and disagreeable, but his brother, Theo, stood by his side, supported his art endeavors, and bailed him out all of the fucking time. At one point, Theo wrote to their younger sister that van Gogh was his own worst enemy and, despite being a gifted artist, he was a fitful, disgruntled man. He sounds like a party.

In 1888, van Gogh ventured to Arles, France in order to schedule some regular, highly productive crafternoons. But he began experiencing incredibly intense mood shifts—he was feverishly creative, then he was listless and exhausted, and he alternated between dysphoria and euphoria. In letters to his brother Theo, van Gogh also referenced having fits of rage, lack of sexual arousal, and being plagued with other physical ailments. Things were definitely sucking. The next story is one we are all familiar with because people really like to tell it: feeling lonesome, van Gogh chatted up his art buddy, Gauguin, and convinced him to come to Arles, but things went south relatively quickly. The tension between the two escalated for various reasons (incompatible personalities, money issues, mental illness, drinking, etc.) and Gauguin decided to leave van Gogh in Arles. But before he had a chance to skip town, van Gogh had a psychotic episode in which he reportedly acted violently towards Gauguin and then cut off part of his own ear. He then proceeded to deliver said ear, or at least a generous piece of it, to his favorite prostitute, Rachel (awww, my name is Rachel, isn't that lovely). Again, all of this is based on information we can't truly verify so we might not be getting our story quite right. Just keep that in mind. This experience marked the beginning of van Gogh's psychotic episodes, which led to a series of hospitalizations. Van Gogh was diagnosed with epilepsy at the time of his treatment and he kept painting away while he was in the hospital and during periods when he was released. His health waxed and waned, his drinking continued, and his brother Theo started moving on with his own life, which caused van Gogh quite a bit of emotional duress. Theo got married and had a kid, and van Gogh was consumed with feelings of abandonment, loneliness, and felt like a burden. At this point in time, van Gogh had been discharged from the hospital and was reportedly "cured," but only ten weeks later, he died by suicide.

Wait. Did van Gogh actually have bipolar disorder? Blumer (2002) sides with doctors and researchers who believe that van Gogh actually had epilepsy and a plethora of other contributing variables, like excessive drinking, brain lesions, environmental concerns, sexually transmitted diseases (cue Rachel), etc. that resulted in the sad story that was his life. However, other people clearly disagree, as evidenced by the bipolar community who is quick to claim van Gogh as our own. My issue here is not actually whether or not epilepsy or bipolar disorder was the cause of van Gogh's self-destructive behavior, his unhealthy decisions, his powerful art, or his abysmal life, because we'll never really know, but rather I want to confront the bipolar community as to why the ill and dysfunctional van Gogh is revered as our bipolar poster child. He seems like a bad choice.

I have bipolar disorder and I ask my similarly afflicted mentally ill sisters, brothers, and non-gendered siblings, why do we love van Gogh so much? In order to get a sense of the answer, I conducted some VERY informal research: I Googled, "Why do people with bipolar love Vincent van Gogh?" These are my crudely summarized results:

1) People identify with his interpersonal struggles: Van Gogh was lonely, at times bullied, excluded, and had a hard time maintaining relationships.

2) People identify with his failures: Van Gogh had a hard time holding down a job, he drank a lot, his art wasn't all that popular when he was alive, he relied entirely on Theo for cash, and his health was crap.

3) People want to identify with his "success:" We attribute van Gogh's creative genius to his illness. *His cyclical suffering was directly responsible for his brilliant masterpieces. Not despite of, but because of his illness, he is an acclaimed great. He was unhappy as hell, but he was a prolific creator. Way to Gogh! Making absinthe out of lemons!*

Vincent van Gogh was misunderstood and underappreciated. Many people living with bipolar disorder can relate to these feelings of isolation, worthlessness, and shame because stigma is a very real part of our lives. Van Gogh was an outcast who was penniless and friendless, but he had an amazing gift. In some ways, this seems like an inherently faulty "overcoming narrative" to me. His artistic gift was lost on most people due to the grip of his vicious, perhaps unidentified, illness. But van Gogh didn't live and die in vain because we still celebrate him and, it feels like, the illness that "inspired" his genius.

And I argue that that is a toxic line of thinking. For starters, I don't think van Gogh's life was actually all that inspiring. His art is magnificent, but he seemed like kind of an asshole. He was irritable, aggressive, a stalker, inconsiderate, manipulative, etc. Van Gogh is not a beacon of hope. In fact, I feel like his only redeeming quality was his artwork, NOT his illness! It is counter intuitive to celebrate the man's illness, because even if it led to his creations, it also killed him. The reason we have a day like today, World Bipolar Day, is to de-stigmatize mental illness so people seek treatment and not succumb to such a vitriolic disease. I have bipolar I disorder and my illness does its best to ruin my life. During my hypomania, mania, psychosis, and depression, I don't oil paint up a storm. I actually don't do anything that makes the illness seemingly "worth it." Seriously, when I'm psychotic, all I do is capsize under the weight of my paranoia, cry uncontrollably, have delusions and obsessions about my teeth, and talk about my guardian angel, Princess Diana. It's a mess, not glamorous.

I get it, bipolar disorder is an illness that severely compromises one's ability to be healthy, happy, and safe. But *owning* the illness is the only way to learn how to live life on your own terms. Yes, living with a mental illness is challenging, and I am not trying to trivialize that struggle. It is even more challenging when you live like van Gogh. But some of us (it is VERY important to note that access to resources and systems is far from equal/equitable for all individuals; people of color living in poverty are systemically silenced, disempowered, marginalized, and tokenized in conversations about mental illness) are fortunate enough to have access to medication and healthcare, supportive networks, opportunities, and thus, the chance to lead fulfilling lives. Our fight against stigma is best won through genuine accomplishments, challenging low expectations, and trying to make the mental health conversation more inclusive and diverse.

I appreciate the artwork of van Gogh and I understand that he struggled, but I refuse to accept him as the emblem of my illness. He was a man who suffered the majority of his existence and he took his own life due to his pain—the only thing that survived was his art. I don't accept that he represents bipolar disorder in the slightest. At least he does not represent what bipolar disorder has to be like today. My hope is not placed in the allegory of a man who was an aloof, brilliant, tortured soul, because it is just not healthy to romanticize his illness. I actively anchor my hope in my own accomplishments, the achievements of my friends who also struggle with mental illness, the love of my friends and family, and the sincere belief that I can make my life better. Something that is way easier to believe and practice when I am not infatuated with the warped appeal of existing as an aloof, brilliant, tortured soul who's definitely doomed. I don't think Vincent van Gogh should be the icon of bipolar disorder. No one person should serve this purpose because this illness is just as unique as the people it impacts, as the independent lives they lead, and as the gifts they each bring to the world when they are healthy. That's true every day, not just on World Bipolar Day.

World Bipolar Day should be about honoring the narratives of people who live with bipolar disorder, confronting stigma, shifting awareness to acceptance, and instilling the hope that if you have bipolar disorder, you can live better and longer than Vincent van Gogh.

Edit: Just in case any World Bipolar Day founders or big wigs at the International Bipolar Foundation stumble upon this book, I wanted to provide a list of other potential bipolar heroes who I would much rather have represent my illness: actress and advocate Carrie Fisher (RIP), comedian Maria Bamford, singer Demi Lovato, musician Kid Cudi, actor Robin Williams (RIP), and revered doctor Kay Redfield Jamison. Let's replace the romanticized narrative of a white, whiny, melancholic, mentally ill, male artist and instead focus on individuals who share their authentic narratives and show that you don't need to be broken to be brilliant. That's my bipolar story.

Blumer, D. (2002). The illness of Vincent van Gogh. *The American Journal of Psychiatry*, 159 (4), 519–526.

the story of trixie pickles and my story of addiction

I adopted Trixie Pickles three weeks ago, and she's the snuggliest dog I've ever had. All she wants out of life is to sit on people's laps, give kisses, and follow my other dogs around and sniff their butts. Trixie Pickles came into our lives unexpectedly. Her owner died of an overdose and she needed a new home, and even though my husband and I already have two dogs and two cats, she's part of the family. What can I say? I also have a big heart.

I've been taking Trixie Pickles all over town to get her used to loud noises, teach her proper dog etiquette when she meets a new butt, show her how to receive pats graciously and not wiggle out of control, and process the crushing blow in self-esteem when people don't want to pet her. I don't speak dog fluently, but I'm assuming – based on squeak frequency and volume – that being turned down for pats is literally the worst thing in the world. Luckily, the majority of people stop me, asking to pet her, and she's more than happy to oblige. Overall, Trixie Pickles is making tremendous progress and she is not afraid to show her new friends how much she cares about them. Cue lots of happy wiggles and squeaks. She's never met an ear scratcher or butt patter or a new face to kiss that she didn't like. And while Trixie Pickles jiggles from one outstretched hand to the next, I find myself chatting to the people giving my dog some TLC.

Oh my god your dog is so cute! I love her ears. Can I pet her?
Thanks for asking. She'd absolutely love that!

What's her name?
Trixie Pickles.

That's so cute! How old is she?
She's a rescue. We think around one.

Still a puppy! Where did you get her from?
It's so sad. Her former owner died of an overdose.

What a terrible person! You're a hero.

In the early stages of walking Trixie Pickles and meeting strangers on the sidewalk, I didn't rehearse my answers ahead of time. I didn't put serious thought into my responses. I just responded truthfully that her owner had died of an overdose. A really sad story that, unfortunately, we're all used to hearing. I didn't even stop to think about what types of reactions there would be to his story, my role as Trixie Pickles's new owner, and the impact all of this has on our cute butterfly-eared squeaker. Lemme tell ya, my privilege has made me so naïve. I soon found that most people had rather passionate opinions about Trixie Pickles's and my situation. I shouldn't have been surprised, but pretty much every person I talked to was quick to make demeaning and demonizing assumptions about her former owner. I know that stigma is real, but I didn't realize how vocal and unabashed people could be. Based on my informal poll of yinzer pedestrians, people who overdose "had it coming." I'm the hero, they're the villain. That's the end of the story.

The opioid epidemic in the United States is tragic and in Pennsylvania drug overdoses are one of the leading causes of accidental death. Drug abuse is everywhere, impacting everyone, and yet people are ready - I'd even say eager- to cast judgment. These informal conversations on curbs and crosswalks have been eye opening. This is the first time I've experienced this firsthand and it shocks me to hear people's opinions. How quickly they fill in the blanks. It's particularly uncomfortable and disheartening because I used to struggle with substance abuse.

I spent well over a decade battling addiction and I've been in recovery for longer. When my anorexia, bipolar, and PTSD converged, I couldn't handle it. There was no way out from being crushed under these illnesses. I started doing drugs to prolong my manic episodes. When you have bipolar I disorder, you want to reside in manic space. Not really, "reside," more like rage, riot, and roar like a euphoric maniac. I thought that manic-me was the best version of me, so I did whatever it took to lose myself in the dangerous throes of mental illness and addiction. Mania was a tantalizing escape. It was definitely scary for a while, but I'm incredibly lucky that I had the resources and support to tackle my addiction issues. I don't take my privilege for granted. Not everyone has the same access to recovery. Not everyone is given the chance to change.

Me and Trixie Pickles. I'm sober and successful. She's cuddly and cute. When I walk down the street, people don't see addiction - they don't expect it. They just see a white woman with an adorable little dog. And it's unsettling how much people praise me for rescuing Trixie Pickles. I get hugs, a free drink at the coffee shop—it's amazing how quickly people make positive assumptions about me. After years of therapy, I've learned how to love myself and how to stay healthy, and shame hasn't been a part of my emotional landscape for years. I was never branded as an addict. I was given the opportunity to take my life back. As I meet new people walking my dog around my city, I can't help but wonder what would change if they knew my story.

Oh my god, your dog is so cute! I love her ears. Can I pet her?
Thanks for asking. She'd absolutely love that!

What's her name?
Trixie Pickles.

That's so cute! How old is she?
She's a rescue. We think around one.

Still a puppy! Where did you get her from?
It's so sad. Her former owner died of an overdose. I can imagine how devastating that must have been. I've struggled with addiction, too.

...

What if that was my answer? What if I told my story? What if I owned my history of addiction and leveraged my privilege to educate others? To confront stigma, leash in-hand? To trade pats for reality checks? To exchange squeaks for storytelling? I wonder if I have the guts to actually have this conversation. And if I managed to muster up the courage to tell my truth, I wonder if my neighborhood dog enthusiasts would judge me. If they would scowl, sigh, and say mean things under their breath. If they'd make negative assumptions about me. If they'd cross the street. If they'd refuse to pet my dog. I think Trixie Pickles and I would both be heartbroken.

fight

For me, bipolar is being lost. I can make out the real world, as blurry as it may be, but it doesn't make sense. I stand with my feet anchored in disorder, looking in and trying to figure out why I don't fit, why I'm stuck on the outskirts where my brain threatens to boil and bubble out of my skull. I'm scared and confused. I hear things that aren't there, the thread of reality unravels, and I'm immobilized in illness. I'm lost and all I want to do is find my way out of my fracturing thoughts and wake up on the side of my mind that's sane. I have to practice mindfulness, nurture hopefulness, and exercise my capacity to truly believe in myself. I have to remind myself over and over that this illness isn't my life.

After writing this book, I've realized that I have a purpose that outshines disease. I'm here not only to make things better for myself, but hopefully for other people with glitchy brains. Bipolar disorder is manipulative and malicious, but we can't let it win. We can come back from the craziness, reclaim our brains, and tip-toe, twirl, strut, sashay, march, roll, and wheel our way back into the real world when we're ready.

Mental illness is both unique and universal.
You are not alone.

Hope, kindness, and compassion are not things we keep for ourselves,
they're things we share.
You will come out the other side.

Without allyship and community, we're all destined to break.
We are in this together.

"When a flower doesn't bloom,
you fix the environment in which it grows, not the flower"
–Alexander Den Heijer
Embrace each others' colors.

CPSIA information can be obtained
at www.ICGtesting.com
Printed in the USA
BVHW022010230220
573082BV00018B/268

9 781944 134204